ABOUT FACE

THE DRAMATIC IMPACT OF THE INTERNET ON POLITICS AND ADVOCACY

Karen A.B. Jagoda

ABOUT FACE

THE DRAMATIC IMPACT OF THE INTERNET ON POLITICS AND ADVOCACY

Karen A.B. Jagoda
Editor and Co-Author

with
HCD Research

Foreword by
Cyrus Krohn

ABOUT FACE

For information contact E-Voter Institute Press

karen@e-voterinstitute.com

Cover illustration and design by Elena Dworkina

First Edition

E-Voter Institute Press

ISBN: 978-0-9825590-0-0

*Enlighten the people generally
and tyranny and oppressions
of body and mind will vanish like
evil spirits at the dawn of day.*

THOMAS JEFFERSON

Contents

Contributors

With thanks to all for their insights, time and willingness to share their experiences. A rising tide surely raises all boats.

Robert K. Arena, Jr.
President, Presage Digital Strategies
presageinc.com

Porter Bayne
Founder, Insight
www.insightapp.cpm

T. A. Berg
President, TABcommunications, inc.
www.TABcommunications.com

Brent Blackaby
Principal & Co-Founder, Blackrock Associates
www.BlackrockOnline.com

Christopher P. Borick
Director, Muhlenberg College Institute of Public Opinion
www.muhlenberg.edu/studorgs/polling/

Mike Connell
Founder, New Media Communications

Corina Constantin, Ph.D.
Director, Didit Labs
www.didit.com

Shaun Dakin
Chief Executive and Founder
Citizens for Civil Discourse, a nonprofit group that has launched the National Political Do Not Contact Registry at StopPoliticalCalls.org.
www.stoppoliticalcalls.org/index.php
@EndTheRoboCalls; @IsCool (Twitter)

Mark Davis
Advisor to Internet and technology businesses
on strategy and business development.
www.markdavis.com/

Colin Delany
Founder and Editor, e.politics
www.epolitics.com

Karen A.B. Jagoda
President and Co-Founder, E-Voter Institute
evoterinstitute.com

Ben Katz
Chief Technology Officer, Aristotle
www.aristotle.com/mos/Contact_Us/task,view/contact_id.73/

Glenn Kessler
CEO , HCD Research
hcdi.net

Jason R. Krebs
President, Sales & Marketing, ShortTail Media, Inc.
www.shorttailmedia.com/about-us/team-shorttail/jason-krebs

Cyrus Krohn
Director of Content Programming, Microsoft
www.msn.com

Kevin Lee
Chairman and CEO/Co-Founder, Didit
www.didit.com

Kathie Legg
Product Manager, National Geographic
facebook.com/kathielegg

Kevin O'Neill
Managing Director, Client Services, Grassroots Enterprise
www.linkedin.com/in/kevinmoneill

Larry Ward
President, Political Media, Inc.
www.politicalmedia.com

Ben Weisberg.
Account Manager, Elections & Issue Advocacy, Google Inc.
google.com

Tony Winders
Vice President, Marketing of ValueClick Media.
www.tonywinders.com

*With special thanks to **Joan Wood** for editing support.*

FOREWORD
CYRUS KROHN

My first encounter with the E-Voter Institute and Karen Jagoda was in 1998 just after the release of their ground-breaking study on the effectiveness of the internet during a political campaign. The study documented how Peter Vallone used online advertising against then Gov. George Pataki. I was employed at Microsoft searching for supporting documentation to help validate the case for shifting traditional advertising dollars to the web as a more efficient and accountable targeting tool for voter contact.

The belief was we could break into an emerging market establishing a sizeable new revenue stream. Leading up to the 2000 presidential election cycle, preparations were made to facilitate this influx. Efforts included establishing political advertising guidelines for the first time and a field sales staff—of one!—to procure dollars. Alas, the floodgates didn't open but we did have some small successes such as selling some of the first online ad space ever to presidential hopefuls [Bradley, McCain] during their 2000 campaigns.

Since that time there have been a number of examples of creative use of the medium -- the majority of which have been studied and documented by the E-Voter Institute. I'm proud to have been a participant in the institute's research efforts over the past 10 years as a contributor, donor and board member.

I'd like to take this opportunity to share some personal insights into the evolution of the intersection of internet and politics; not as a researcher, but practitioner. I became so enamored with the subject I opted to leave a comfortable private sector job to join the Republican National Committee in mid 2007 to gear up for the 2008 presidential election and practice what I had been preaching. The research and personal connections established through the E-Voter Institute over the previous decade were a great help to me. This book is one more effort towards documenting a continually evolving industry. As President Obama and his online operatives will attest, the internet is important.

The E-Voter Institute's 2000 study included a piece by Max Fose, former internet director for John McCain's failed 1999 campaign. It's ironic that Sen. McCain's campaign was one of the first to use the internet so effectively for online fundraising and communication only to be outdone 8 years later, albeit with the help of Facebook co-founder Chris Jones. In the 2000 study Mr. Fose highlights the campaigns online metrics. "We raised over $6.4 million online alone and that shocked everybody", said Fose, who also noted the campaign accrued over 142,000 e-mail addresses. These figures are now commonplace in presidential campaigns with the difference being these metrics are attainable over 24 hours rather than 52 weeks.

In that same study there were predictions made about the future of political campaigns. Joe Sandler, a middle-aged strategist and 25 year veteran of Democrat politics, offered some educated guesses on where we'd be in 2010. His insights were prescient. The one area he predicted would come of age but is still in its infancy is the evolution of national voter files for strategic use online.

During the 2008 presidential election the Democrats chose to outsource their data needs to Catalyst, a recently formed data aggregator by Harold Ickes, a longtime confidant of the Clintons. The GOP maintains their national voter file database within the Republican National Committee headquarters and is commonly known as "Voter Vault". The GOP once boasted superiority in its use of database technology and it was superior in its time according to numerous press articles.

Now the Democrats appear to have surpassed the Republicans and by choosing to house the database outside the political party headquarters it has freed them from some of the election law hurdles. As an example,

Catalyst and MoveOn.org collaborated to create a web-based application and website at VotePoke.com that was 1-click access to retrieve data to encourage friends to register to vote or change party affiliation in almost real-time. The RNC opted to overlay their voter files on top of major publishers databases identifying likely voters by party affiliation and serving advertisements to their computers knowing precisely who we were reaching. In fact, 76% of the voters who clicked on an ad voted.

This is the second volume from the E-Voter Institute. Two essays written by me were included in the first volume, **Crossing the River: The Coming of Age of the Internet in Politics and Advocacy** (Xlibris 2005). One of the chapters was titled **Hunting Buffalo: Finding New Enthusiasts in their Natural Environment** and was written along with Todd Herman, who is the current e-Campaign Director of the Republican National Committee.

As we celebrate the 10-year anniversary of the founding of the E-Voter institute and look forward to the 2010 mid-term elections, I expect this publication will stand the test of time and serve as a guide for ongoing elections another decade from now. The small community of online political operatives has grown considerably and with it new ideas and creative approaches to the medium. I suspect in four years we'll be focusing our attention on mobile devices and the continuing importance these devices are having on the political process. But that is material for the next E-Voter Institute book.

PART I
Expectations

CHAPTER 1

Knowledge is Power: Web 3.0 and Online Political Communications

Karen A.B. Jagoda

About Face

As we were putting this book together, the election in Iran was taking place and social networks, Twitter and YouTube became the primary sources of information to the outside world about the protests that followed. This further confirmed the perception that the Internet has indeed turned the world inside out.

This book marks the end of the Web 2.0 world where politicians, advocates, and their consultants and media advisors can be content with a false sense of control, and a view that the established means of communicating with constituents is still working albeit with some interactivity facilitated by the web.

Why the title? About face in three ways:

- Political consultants have made an about face on the need to incorporate the web in their campaign strategies.
- Campaigns as never before are more about the authentic face of the candidate or advocate with digital capture devices everywhere.
- With the advent of social networks, it is increasingly about the faces of the voters and supporters and how they interact with the campaign and each other.

This book includes evidence from 2008 of what we now know was a significant turning point in the recognition that the web is here to stay in political and advocacy campaigns and that voters are forever changed in how they think about candidates and causes.

We focus on three key questions:

- What do voters expect?
- What does a modern political or advocacy campaign look like?
- What are the best ways to spend money on the Internet to multiply and enhance the value of dollars spent on traditional media such as television, cable, and radio ads, direct mail, phone banks, and yard signs?

The book traces the most important trends in this environment including:

- The message and the messenger-- authenticity, awareness, and action
- Building community--the power of social media and the rise of the unofficial campaign
- Advertising, search, and email—targeting constituents, contributors, and voters

Historical View

E-Voter Institute, founded in 1999, is a non-partisan trade association whose mission is to help accelerate the use of the Internet for politics and advocacy to support a more robust democracy.

In some small ways the Institute has influenced the growth of the industry of online political communications beginning with the groundbreaking *E-Voter 98 Study* which demonstrated the potential of online banner ads for political persuasion. In addition to our ongoing research, events and webcasts have facilitated discussions between and amongst those of opposing parties, competing web sites, and traditional media and Internet experts. This book is a non-partisan review of innovations and best practices from political and advocacy campaigns with the goal of accelerating the use of these tools in national, state and local races in the next election cycles.

Published in 2005, *Crossing the River: The Coming of Age of the Internet in Politics and Advocacy,* editor Karen A.B. Jagoda (Xlibris, 2005), is a collection of survey data and essays from noted authorities on the early years of this emerging industry. Many of these early adopters and thought leaders went on to work in political and advocacy campaigns, with web publishers to sell ad inventory and other Internet solutions, manage Internet strategy for national campaign committees, and start companies based on the evidence that change was coming.

Contributors

What follows are essays by those who provided and used political online tools including advertising, email, search, video, social networks and a variety of research techniques. Insiders all, the writers have seen the adaptation of the Internet in politics and advocacy over the last decade. As a group they provide clarity to the subject, and as individual experts, they bring wisdom to the best practices and predictions they offer. Authors have been identified in each chapter, sources have been identified for illustrations, and the rest is E-Voter Institute research.

E-Voter Institute and HCD Research

Since 2000, E-Voter Institute has conducted surveys of political and advocacy communications leaders to track their perceptions of how effective the Internet was for fundraising, reaching the base, persuasion, and getting out the vote. In 2006, it became obvious that the Internet was attracting enough of a mass audience to consider it representative of general voters and to make the web a serious contender for attracting advertising dollars. All that was needed was proof that money spent online could get a candidate elected or even just make the difference in a close race.

The first step was to find out more about how voters acted online. While advertisers for consumer goods and business services have developed media optimization models to reach very specific audiences, the denial that the Internet represented "real" voters delayed the education of the political consultants responsible for media budgets.

Beginning in 2006, E-Voter Institute also started surveying voters of all ages across the U.S. with the support of HCD Research using both their panels and online outreach through support of partners. We have included E-Voter Institute research from the summer of 2008 as well as from the survey of voters post election November 2008. In many cases we compare changes from earlier surveys.

These surveys of voters reveal significant trends in web-based searches for information about candidates, where to contribute and how to volunteer for campaigns. There was also a startling difference in the way political consultants generally viewed the effectiveness of web tools versus what voters were using.

The chapter on methodology provides more background on how the surveys were conducted and who responded to the surveys. Specific E-Voter Institute research findings are included throughout the book.

Changes Ahead

Our goal for all readers is to find a way to relate to the changes that are taking place in the political scene in order to enhance a campaign, help refine a campaign strategy, better understand the political trends, or add data to the universe of campaign stories about how candidates won or why they lost.

The number of people who accept and support the use of the Internet in political campaigns has noticeably grown. We also hope that those advisors who are still questioning the role of web tools in the political landscape will find compelling information that encourages them to experiment, and to think more creatively about using the Internet to multiply the impact of dollars spent on other media.

The mosaic of elements in a modern campaign have been altered as candidates and consultants struggle with integrating the Internet dimension into the traditional campaign tactics of television, direct mail and phone banks. As the era of Web 3.0 dawns, consultants will see the need to better understand the interests of individual and dynamic segments of their constituents. The one size fits all days of campaigns are over.

While Web 1.0 was about a basic campaign brochure and a place for supporters to contribute, Web 2.0 allowed for interaction between candidates and constituents as well as peer-to-peer exchanges between supporters and advocates. What we are seeing from the races in 2008 is the change in voter expectations and how citizens interact with candidates, elected officials, and government agencies.

We predict that the growth of Web 3.0 will be influenced by the ways in which the Internet engages people across the political spectrum. While it might be desirable and possible to get passionate supporters for a popular consumer brand, the passion aroused by political leaders, advocates and their supporters in a cause or campaign is what really shifts the way society, online and offline, functions.

What happens when despite all the money that is raised, a candidate still cannot break through to voters? When will voters stop sending buckets of money unconditionally to candidates just because they ask and start asking where all that money is going? Most interesting is how will the unofficial campaign alter the insiders' game?

The E-Voter Institute research on political consultants continues to show that the consultants are becoming less hesitant to use the web to reach voters but they are still thinking about elections as a one-day sale with the web as a convenient ATM for getting money from voters in response to some attack or goal.

Of course not all political strategists, pollsters, media advisors, public relations professionals, fundraisers, grassroots organizers, and campaign strategists are afraid of the changes being brought about by the web. But even those who have educated themselves or hired those who know how to use online tools are still looking over their shoulders to see who is gaining on them.

Iranians riot over vote count
Ahmadinejad claims victory; rival reportedly under house arrest
By Borzou Daragahi for the Los Angeles Times June 14, 2009

"Video showing unrest in the city of Shiraz emerged early today, but reports of other outbreaks could not be confirmed as authorities tried to limit the scale of the demonstrations by curtailing electronic communications. Websites such as Facebook and YouTube, available during the campaign were suddenly filtered. For hours Saturday, the Tehran cell phone network was shut down...Local news reports did not mention the protests or the claims of fraud by the Mousavi campaign."

Tehran, Iran CNN.com June 20, 2009

Moussavi seemed to be encouraging demonstrators to continue their protests with messages posted on his page on Facebook, the social networking Web site that has proven to be a key source of information in the absence of international media coverage.

"Today you are the media," said one message. "It is your duty to report and keep the hope alive."

Iran's ruling system is "going to the slaughterhouse," a post on the site said.

The post, attributed to Moussavi, reasserted his call for a new election to be overseen by an independent council.

Earlier in the day, Moussavi declared on Facebook that he was ready for "martyrdom." That message urged his supporters to "protest" and "not go to work."

Iranian Leaders Gaining the Edge Over Protesters-Challenger Backs Off But President's Tenure May Be Rocky as Foes Bide Time
Nazila Fathi and Michael Slackman
New York Times June 27, 2009 Page 1

While protestors were aided at first by technology--primarily the Internet and text messaging--the government deployed its control of state television and news outlets to sweep away competing narratives.

"It is still possible that the information age will crack authoritarian structures in Iran," wrote Jon B. Alterman, director of the Middle East program for the Center for Strategic and International Studies in Washington. "But it is far more likely that the government will be able to use that technology to secure its own rule."

Iranian paper calls for Mousavi to face trial
In response, the opposition figure details his allegations of voting irregularities
By Borzou Daragahi for the Los Angles Times July 5, 2009

A right-wing newspaper close to Iran's supreme leader on Saturday accused the country's main opposition figure of being a dupe for Iran's foreign enemies and said he should face trial.

But Mir-Hossein Mousavi, defeated presidential candidate and leader of a nascent reform movement, remained unbowed. The soft-spoken but defiant former prime minister responded by releasing his most detailed account yet of what he maintains was vote-rigging and irregularities in last month's reelection of President Mahmoud Ahmadinehad, including an allegation that only the incumbent's allies were allowed to witness vote-counting on election day.

"None of the (opposition) candidates' representatives were allowed to go in," states the three-part report, posted on his website, ghalamnews.ir.

CHAPTER 2

Methodology: E-Voter Institute and HCD Research Surveys 2006-2008

Karen A.B. Jagoda

Introduction

Since the ground breaking E-Voter '98 study which showed that online advertising had the potential to persuade voters, the E-Voter Institute has continued to delve into how the political and advocacy communications leaders are positioning the Internet in their media strategies.

This research is intended to help candidates, campaigns, political consultants, media advisors, fundraisers, pollsters, campaign solution providers, web publishers, online ad networks, academics and journalists better understand the impact of the Internet in the campaign process.

Research partner for the E-Voter Institute surveys was HCD Research, a marketing and communications research company that was founded in 1991. HCD Research focuses solely on providing traditional and e-based marketing and communications research services. The company's web-based research combines classical and sophisticated research techniques with innovative on-line applications that enable HCD Research to obtain comprehensive, meaningful data for customers.

A pioneer in Internet marketing and communications research, HCD Research has designed and implemented research studies for numerous large and mid-sized companies in the pharmaceutical, financial services and publishing industries, among others. HCD Research is also the developer of readmylipz.com, a political ad testing web site for the 2004 Presidential campaign. Rich Berke is vice president, Kendall Anderson was the project manager and Michelle Lambert, research analyst for these surveys. For more information, please visit www. hcdi.net

Joining the research analysis team was Christopher Borick, the Director of the Muhlenberg College, Institute of Public Opinion, a state of the art public opinion research center that conducts scientific based survey research projects of public policy and political issues throughout the Commonwealth of Pennsylvania. See www.muhlenberg.edu/studorgs/polling

Methodology for Summer 2008 Surveys

Participating organizations ran online ad banners and text links on their websites to attract respondents for the Annual Surveys of Political and Advocacy Communications Leaders. In addition, emails were sent to membership lists, client lists, and newsletter recipients to request participation in the survey. The 2008 surveys ran from May 13, 2008 to June 3, 2008. No survey respondents were paid for their answers.

HCD Research adheres to the highest panel recruitment and management standards. Members are enrolled using online recruitment methods (email requests, online banners and blog ads), exclusively using permission-based techniques. The surveys were hosted on the HCD server. HCD Research maintained privacy and all answers stripped of any identifying information. No emails were collected from survey respondents.

In 2006, there were 155 consultants in the sample and in 2007, 230 consultants participated. In 2008, a total sample size of 178 consultants was obtained. Details follow on the 2008 survey sample.

The distribution in 2008 survey across types of clients and years in business:

% of Consultants Who Work for the Following Organizations	
Democratic candidates	60%
Republican candidates	35%
Independent candidates	21%
PACs or Trade Associations	31%
527 Committees	22%
Unions	28%
For-Profit businesses	34%
Not-For-Profit organizations	58%
Organizations outside the U.S.	8%

% Consultants Years Experience	
Less than 1	4%
1-5	22%
6-15	30%
16-25	20%
26-35	13%
More than 35	11%

E-Voter Institute 2008 Seventh Annual Survey of Political and Advocacy Communications Leaders

To recruit respondents for the Annual Surveys of Voter Expectations, participating organizations ran online ad banners and text links on their websites to attract respondents. Additionally, emails were sent to membership lists and HCD's online panel. The 2008 survey ran from May 8, 2008 to May 28, 2008. No survey respondents were paid for their answers.

Respondents to the voter survey were randomly selected from a panel of over 250,000 people who have opted-in and agreed to participate in research. Potential panelists were selected via a random sample obtained through postal mailings directed to individuals on voter registration lists and registrants from websites representing lifestyle, politics, and news organizations.

In 2006, 1033 voters participated in the First Annual Survey of Voter Expectations and in 2007, 1609 voters replied to the Second Annual Survey.

There were a total of 4801 survey respondents in the sample from the 2008 Voters Expectation survey. Some key points of distribution follow.

Voters by Age by Gender			
Age	Total	Males	Females
18-24	10%	14%	8%
25-34	26%	28%	25%
35-54	49%	42%	52%
55-64	12%	12%	13%
65-74	2%	3%	2%
75+	1%	1%	1%

E-Voter Institute 2008 Third Annual Survey of Voter Expectations

Methodology for Post-Election Survey

To recruit respondents for the E-Voter Institute's 2008 Post-Election Study, emails were sent to an online panel through HCD Research. The survey ran from November 5, 2008 to November 10, 2008. No survey respondents were paid for their answers.

Respondents to the voter survey were randomly selected from a panel of people who have opted-in and agreed to participate in research. HCD Research adheres to the highest panel recruitment and management standards. Members are enrolled using online recruitment methods (email requests, online banners and blog ads), exclusively using permission-based techniques. The surveys were hosted on the HCD server. HCD Research maintained privacy and all answers were stripped of any identifying information.

There were 3536 respondents to the E-Voter Institute survey conducted right after the November 2008 election by HCD Research.

The characteristics of that group are as follows:

Gender	
Male	32%
Female	68%
Age	
18-24 years old	9%
25-34 years old	25%
35-54 years old	47%
55-64 years old	14%
65-74 years old	4%
75+ years old	1%
Ethnic Mix	
Caucasian	81%
African-American	7%
Asian	6%
Hispanic	4%
Other/Prefer not to answer	2%

Voters	
Voted at the polls	73%
Voted mail-in or absentee	18%
Didn't vote but were over 18 years of age	9%

Of Those Who Voted	
Always vote in all elections	74%
Only vote in general elections	14%
Vote sometimes	6%
Were first time voters	5%

E-Voter Institute 2008 Post Election Survey of Voter Expectations

Party Affiliation	
Democrats	43%
Republicans	28%
Independents	23%
Libertarian	1%
Prefer not to answer	5%
Self-Described Position Along the Political Spectrum	
Very or somewhat liberal	34%
Moderate	37%
Very or somewhat conservative	29%
Self-Described Level of Political Activism	
Very politically active	17%
Occasionally active in politics	41%
Not engaged in political activities other than voting	42%

E-Voter Institute 2008 Post Election Survey of Voter Expectations

CHAPTER 3

The Winner in 2008?
Online Politics

Mike Connell

"...The credit belongs to the man who is actually in the arena, whose face is marred by dust and sweat and blood; who strives valiantly; who errs, who comes short again and again, because there is no effort without error and shortcoming..." **Teddy Roosevelt**

One of my favorite quotes is Teddy Roosevelt's "Man in the Arena." And coming out of the 2008 election cycle, I'm feeling like my face has been particularly marred, my knuckles exceptionally bruised. As the dust clears, one must look back and ask,"What did the Internet really accomplish in the 2008 election cycle?"

In spite of the vote tallies, this was truly a big election cycle for the Internet.

The fact that the Internet played a critical role in this election is undeniable. What is noteworthy is how it played a different role. You see, in 1996, 2000, and 2004, technological advancement was defined by new techniques, technologies and innovation. In spite of all the buzz about Facebook, YouTube and social media in general, what made 2008 monumental was not the development of new Internet technologies, but rather the integration of that technology into the overall campaign.

Pure and simple, 2008 was about execution. This is the year that the online strategy truly became integrated into the campaign plan. For years, we've preached the need for making the Internet the backbone of the campaign operation and 2008 is the first year where that level of integration began to truly emerge.

In spite of whether your candidate won or lost, the Internet is truly the big winner of 2008. And this is good news for New Media Communications, as the demand for those who understand both politics and technology will continue to escalate. Here's to 2010!

From the Christmas 2008 Newsletter sent by Mike Connell, founder of New Media Communications. He was killed in a plane crash December 19, 2008.

CHAPTER 4

How the Web is Changing Voter Expectations

Karen A.B. Jagoda

E-Voter Institute has noted over the last 3 years the growing influence of the Internet on how voters get their information about candidates and causes and how they make voting decisions. It is the political consultants who seem to be lagging behind in their understanding about how voters' media habits have changed

In the E-Voter Institute May 2008 survey of Voter Expectations, 52% of those who intended to vote expected an official web site. Only 25% of the consultants think web sites are effective for reaching the loyal base and 22% believe they are useful to reach swing, Independent and undecided voters.

One out of four who intended to vote expected to see online ads while only 5% of the consultants thought online ads are effective for reaching the loyal base and 11% thought they work with swing, Independent and undecided voters.

Voter Expectations vs. Consultants View of What Works						
		Intent to Vote			Who Consultants Think Web is Effective For	
Web Activities	Total Voters	Yes	No	Not Sure	Loyal Base	Others
Official web site	87%	89%	73%	83%	25%	22%
E-mail	60%	62%	48%	50%	46%	13%
Online ads	65%	66%	54%	58%	5%	11%
Webcasts of events	62%	64%	53%	52%	4%	3%
Blogs and podcasts	55%	56%	43%	48%	8%	4%
Web video on other sites	60%	61%	48%	54%	7%	11%
Social Net Site	38%	39%	32%	31%	10%	11%

E-Voter Institute 2008 Third Annual Survey of Voter Expectations and Seventh Annual Survey of Political and Advocacy Communications Leaders

Voter Expectations by Gender and Party

E-Voter Institute 2008 research reveals that a solid majority of voters expect political candidates to utilize Internet technology to maintain an official web site, raise money and place their television ads online. Close behind are online ads and webcasts.

Men generally have higher expectations about how candidates should use the web but 87%, the same proportion of men as women, expect an official campaign web site. The most significant difference in gender expectations is over participation in social networking sites with men 25% more likely to expect the social network presence.

Voter Expectations of Candidates						
		Intent to Vote			Gender	
Web Activities	Total	Yes	No	Not Sure	M	F
Official web site	87%	89%	73%	83%	87%	87%
Fund raising	70%	72%	53%	60%	75%	68%
Television ads on the official web site	68%	70%	56%	61%	71%	67%
Online ads	65%	66%	54%	58%	68%	63%
Webcasts of events	62%	64%	53%	52%	64%	62%
E-mail	60%	62%	48%	50%	65%	58%
Campaign web video on other sites	60%	61%	48%	54%	63%	58%
Blogs and podcasts	55%	56%	43%	48%	59%	53%
Social Net Sites	38%	39%	32%	31%	45%	36%

E-Voter Institute 2008 Third Annual Survey of Voter Expectations

Those self-identified as Democrats expect more use of email and participation in social networks than Republicans and Independents. When we break out self-identified Power Users, even more differences in expectations emerge and we see a significant increase in expectations for email, online ads, webcasts and candidate commercials posted online.

Voter Expectations of Candidates	Dem	Rep	Ind
Official web site	89%	87%	88%
Fund raising	73%	68%	72%
E-mail	65%	56%	59%
Online ads	67%	65%	63%
Webcasts of events	65%	61%	62%
Blogs and podcasts	57%	51%	57%
Television ads on the official web site	71%	68%	68%
Campaign web video on other sites	62%	58%	60%
Social Net Site	43%	33%	37%

E-Voter Institute 2008 Third Annual Survey of Voter Expectations

Voters and Technology

Voters are tech savvy with a broad acceptance of Internet tools. As expected, those highly politically active are more likely to take action online.

The E-Voter Institute 2008 Third Annual Survey of Voter Expectations showed that a vast majority of voters use email and make online purchases. Two out of three people forward links and email to friends and family and read newspapers online. Over half play online games and download video and/or audio. Three quarters have broadband access at home and 50% have wireless capability.

Those who are most politically active show less interest in email and significantly more interest in posting ratings or comments and downloading video or audio. Those who are not engaged in political activities other than voting show the least interest in online newspapers, downloading and uploading video, posting comments and ratings and blogging. They are also the least likely to be members of an online social network.

Characteristics of Voters By Self-Described Level of Political Activism				
Online Activities	Total	Very active	Not very active	Not active other than voting
Use email	92%	85%	92%	94%
Make online purchases	79%	75%	81%	78%
Forward links and email to friends/family	69%	68%	71%	67%
Read newspapers or magazines online	66%	73%	74%	58%
Play online games	57%	55%	61%	55%
Download video and/or audio	53%	62%	60%	45%
Post ratings or comments online	46%	57%	53%	37%
Listen to online radio	44%	55%	50%	36%
Social network member	44%	53%	49%	37%
Upload video and/or audio	33%	42%	40%	25%
Post to other blogs	28%	45%	34%	19%
Use widgets	19%	27%	22%	14%
Maintain a blog or your own web site	19%	29%	22%	13%
Subscribe to RSS feeds	18%	30%	21%	12%
Use Twitter or other micro-blogging sites	5%	15%	5%	2%

E-Voter Institute 2008 Third Annual Survey of Voter Expectations

Technology Competence

When it comes to the levels of comfort with new technology, online technology competence is more a factor of age and gender than party affiliation. Breakout by level of online technology competence and party affiliation shows fairly consistent distributions but evaluating based on gender and age shows a different story.

- 84% more men than women consider themselves Power Users
- The percentage of Power Users drops off with age
- 50% of those 55+ consider themselves competent in basic online technology

Technology Competence of Voters by Party				
	Total	Dem	Rep	Ind
Power User - Staying on the leading edge of the Internet	24%	25%	24%	22%
Advanced - Maintaining awareness of changes in online technology	46%	46%	45%	48%
Competent - Satisfied with basic online technology to get the job done	28%	27%	29%	28%
Novice - Limited ability to take advantage of all online technology	3%	2%	2%	3%

E-Voter Institute 2008 Third Annual Survey of Voter Expectations

PART II
The Message
and The Messengers

CHAPTER 5

Politics in a New Age of Authenticity

Robert K. Arena, Jr.

In 2008, the key to online success of the Presidential election was authenticity - authenticity of speech and communications, authenticity of proposed new policies from prospective leaders, and authenticity of participation by the electorate. Authenticity is a difficult thing in the grand scale of politics - it's about honesty and accuracy, generally not attributes of politics. Furthermore, many of our political judgments aren't about just accuracy of facts and truthfulness - politics is also about the gut measure of a man or a woman seeking office. Digital technology was key to providing the intimacy of a personal interaction with the candidates to help voters make those ever-important gut judgments.

Technology isn't generally viewed as a particularly intimate medium of communications, but that is due more to a lack of vision than a lack of capability. In 2008, the Internet came into its own as an intimate medium of communications, not just one of information. Candidates and groups alike found that voters and constituencies took to the Internet in droves. What voters sought out wasn't just press release or a replay of a 30 second TV commercial - they really sought a way to participate in the democracy on their terms in an authentic way.

After eight years of tightly managed communications and spin from leaders who rarely subjected themselves to the questions of the media (let alone the governed), the public was ready to dive into politics once again. In 2004, Howard Dean had whetted their appetite for a plain speaking approach to politics that reminded voters that if they participated in their government they would make it more accountable - government was a product of its citizens, they ultimately held the power. If an imperfect messenger himself, the message stuck. What did Howard Dean do?

The birth of YouTube in 2005, coupled with the aggregated audiences of blogs created a perfect storm to prove this point. In 2006, the routine video capture of a candidate speaking "off the cuff" at an event on the campaign trail tipped the balance of power in the United States Senate.

As most everyone is well aware now, George Allen's "maccaca" moment was the proof of the concept that for an image to be believable you can only craft it so far off from your true self. No matter how much money you raise, no matter how many people you buy off, no matter how well entrenched, when the real George Allen finally emerged into the clear, it was obvious that the carefully crafted image Allen had been building for decades was merely a facade on a hateful person. Virginia voters had enough;[1] as had voters across the nation - pulling control of both Houses of Congress out from under President Bush. The foundation politics had been built on had shifted and the 2008 Presidential season was about to begin.

Total Spending by Presidential Candidates*

Total Spent

Year		Total
2008[1]		$1,324.7
2004		$717.9
2000		$343.1
1996		$239.9
1992		$192.2
1988		$210.7
1984		$103.6
1980		$92.3
1976		$66.9

Monthly U.S. People 07/02/06 - 02/28/09 — Directly Measured ····· Rough Estimate

youtube.com

● US 80.0M Max: 82.0M 04/16/08

In 2007 and 2008, YouTube moved from being simply a distribution of campaign commercials into a critical and integral part of the campaign apparatus. Campaign channels began to regularly include full speeches by candidates, web-only ad replies, state specific volunteer coordinating videos, and celebrities visiting campaign HQs to make phone calls. And voters loved it. By the end of the Presidential election, viewing hours to Obama's and McCain's YouTube channel totaled 14.5 million and 500,000 hours respectively.[2] Whether it was the candidates giving a speech on a thorny issue or the operative instructing voters on how to get involved in the campaign, online video was about looking someone in the eye and the viewer judging them. Is this candidate telling the truth? Am I really going to take off a weekend with my friends to go door to door for a candidate? Will my time be well utilized?

With the higher emotional engagement of video often used in conjunction with email appeals, the number of donors substantially increased in the 2008 cycle as did the total amount of money spent.[3] While money in politics has been viewed in highly negative terms, in 2008 we found the resurgence of the power of the small donor. Obama, the younger, less well-connected politician, took on the powers within his party and lacking the traditional fundraising apparatus of a more seasoned candidate, went out and built a new apparatus from scratch using online tools. Obama's authenticity was met by donors willing to put their money behind the campaign - to the extreme that Obama was able to opt out of public financing and change the entire Presidential landscape - raising an astonishing $745 million.[4]

The great thing about getting people to part with their money to support a candidate is that it takes them from passive observer to active participant. Having donated and feeling a more direct connection to the outcome of the race, campaigns quickly capitalized on the opportunity to get those voters more involved. Whether it was phone-banking or door-to-door canvassing, the goal of these efforts was to have real people talking to real people - get the campaigns out of the spin machine and back to basics.

MyBarackObama.com was the ultimate example of bringing authenticity directly into the political persuasion process.[5] Using the Internet, the Obama campaign was able to facilitate face to face communication with actual neighbors in states like Virginia, North Carolina, Colorado - places where Democrats have been afraid to show their faces for too long.

Even in places where volunteers didn't feel comfortable going door to door, MyBarackObama.com gave volunteers the support they needed to phone-bank to other states or instructions on how to execute a person-to-person postcard campaign. In the end, over 8,000,000 calls were made by volunteers to undecided voters using the tools built into MyBarackObama.com.[6]

Digitally engaged voters are also a great avenue for countering negative messages.[7] For such a long time, too much of our politics was taken up by the very impersonal direct mail and robo-call culture of prior elections. If you felt really desperate or really gutsy, you could try putting it on television, but the media backlash generated often meant much of that material was relegated to the less overt direct channels.

The objective was simple - stuff a distracting negative message about your opponent down the throat of the voter over the last week of the election. It even had a fancy, neutered name - voter suppression.

In a late minute development in the North Carolina Senate race in 2008, Elizabeth Dole's trailing campaign accused her opponent, Kay Hagan, of being a "godless" American because she attended a fundraiser with an atheist.[8] The ad, dropped late in the game, got immediate attention given the historical context of smear ads in North Carolina politics.

But unlike past attempts, this last minute tactic backfired. Kay Hagan was far from a "godless" woman - she was a volunteer Sunday School teacher. On top of that, the Dole ad implied at its close that Hagan said "there is no god" - clearly a less than genuine edit.

The Hagan campaign responded initially in the press and with blogs. Then the campaign cut a response ad - "Belief" extremely quickly - strongly defending Hagen. The blogs picked up the response ad and the media followed with a fresh round of attention. The "sunshine" on the Dole ad gave Hagan an opportunity to prove Dole wasn't an authentic leader, but a politician willing to say anything.

When voters got to look at the two candidates side-by-side, one was hiding behind a false charge and the other was looking right at the voter and defending herself. Hagan won the race easily in a state not know to be overly friendly to Democrats.

The Internet ultimately enabled the 2008 political cycle to become a much more authentic campaign than we've experienced in decades. After years of talk about the first Presidential campaign truly enabled by the Internet, we finally saw it happen. Due to the internet, the public took to the political process in ways that we've only talked about academically - they donated, volunteered, and voted in record numbers and brought forth a political reality. No matter whether you agree with the outcome of the election, there is no denying that the Internet has ushered in a rejuvenated era of American politics.

---

1. Chart source www.quantcast.com/youtube.com#traffic
2. www.newsweek.com/id/168269/output/print
3. Spending in millions - chart source www.opensecrets.org/pres08/totals.php?cycle=2008
4. www.opensecrets.org/pres08/summary.php?id=N00009638
5. Image credit: www.progressillinois.com/files/images/group.jpg
6. www.fastcompany.com/node/1207594/print
7. Screen grab: www.youtube.com/watch?v=6JkxTv4SQww
8. Screen grab: www.youtube.com/watch?v=k76tRXq0ZC0

CHAPTER 6

Getting
a Message Heard

Karen A.B. Jagoda

According to the E-Voter Institute Third Annual Survey of Voter Expectations, television and cable advertising, debates and official candidate web sites are the most effective methods for getting the attention of voters.

When asked what are the best ways to get their attention, ten percent more Democrats than Republicans pay attention to official web sites and emails from candidates. Independents are the most likely to respond to word of mouth and are 50% more likely to be paying attention to independent blog postings than Republicans.

As we suspected, young voters between the ages of 18-34 are more likely to be influenced by Internet information than those over 35. It is interesting to note however that

- effectiveness of email from candidate or celebrity increases with age
- webcasts are compelling to those 18-64
- nearly 50% of those 35-64 rely on official web sites
- yard signs get the attention of 18-24 year olds as much as those 35-54

- debates attract 58% of those 18-24, about the same number of those 35+

A little historical perspective leads us to conclude that it is becoming increasingly hard to get voters' attention. In each category there is noticeable drop off in the number of people who say that any specific method is a good way to reach them. Unfortunately, we did not ask about debates last year, as it appears they are the second most popular way to get voters attention in 2008. We will watch this trend in future surveys.

Best Ways to Get Voters' Attention-By Party				
Activities	Total	Dem	Rep	Ind
Television or cable ads	63%	68%	61%	58%
Debates	57%	61%	55%	58%
Official web site	51%	56%	46%	49%
Word of mouth	39%	40%	35%	42%
Direct mail	31%	36%	32%	27%
Newspaper ads	29%	33%	28%	26%
Radio ads	26%	28%	26%	22%
Online ads	25%	28%	22%	23%
E-mail from candidate or celebrity endorser	22%	28%	18%	19%
Webcasts	20%	22%	17%	21%
Yard signs, outdoor billboards	20%	23%	19%	15%
Independent blog posting	16%	17%	12%	18%
Social networking sites	15%	17%	11%	15%
Viral video about a candidate	14%	17%	11%	14%
Phone	9%	11%	8%	7%
Text messaging	5%	5%	4%	4%

E-Voter Institute 2008 Third Annual Survey of Voter Expectations

Best Ways to Get Voters' Attention-By Age

Activities	18-24	25-34	35-54	55-64	65-74	75+
Television or cable ads	57%	60%	64%	67%	70%	54%
Direct mail	24%	30%	31%	39%	42%	36%
Online ads	29%	28%	24%	21%	18%	11%
E-mail from candidate or celebrity endorser	20%	22%	22%	23%	31%	11%
Newspaper ads	24%	27%	30%	34%	41%	29%
Social networking sites	28%	22%	12%	9%	7%	4%
Phone	7%	10%	8%	9%	14%	4%
Official web site	53%	55%	51%	46%	33%	25%
Viral video about a candidate	27%	16%	12%	10%	10%	11%
Radio ads	24%	28%	26%	25%	23%	14%
Webcasts	18%	22%	20%	18%	9%	11%
Debates	58%	54%	57%	60%	66%	50%
Independent blog posting	23%	20%	15%	11%	5%	4%
Text messaging	6%	6%	4%	3%	0%	0%
Yard signs and outdoor billboards	19%	22%	19%	18%	18%	14%
Word of mouth	57%	46%	36%	30%	30%	7%

E-Voter Institute 2008 Third Annual Survey of Voter Expectations

Best Ways to Get Voters' Attention		
Activities	2007 Voters	2008 Voters
Television or cable ads	64%	63%
Debates	N/A	57%
Official web site	53%	51%
Word of mouth	48%	39%
Direct mail	37%	31%
Newspaper ads	35%	29%
Radio ads	35%	26%
Online ads	30%	25%
E-mail from candidate or celebrity endorser	36%	22%
Webcasts	21%	20%
Yard signs and outdoor billboards	29%	20%
Independent blog posting	N/A	16%
Social networking sites	24%	15%
Viral video about a candidate	N/A	14%
Phone	12%	9%
Text messaging	10%	5%

E-Voter Institute 2008 Third Annual Survey of Voter Expectations

Ellen Johnson Sirleaf, President of Liberia tells a story in her autobiography *This Child Will Be Great: Memoir of a Remarkable Life by Africa's First Woman President* (Harper and Collins, 2009) about how her party spent $2 million on the campaign and they were far from the top spenders.

She relates that in earlier campaigns, candidates went to a house or a town or a village, and the people provided accommodations and food, and maybe even put a bit of money in the pot for travel and gas. By 2005, however, the electorate was in no mood to give and they wanted things. President Sirleaf says this in large part was an outgrowth of the war and the poverty it had engendered and people simply no longer had enough to give.

But she points out, "They also knew that the competition meant goodies for them, so they expected goodies from everybody: T-shirts, caps, footballs, and bags and bags of rice. One really had to do it. T-shirts were especially popular, because they were clothing and could be worn and worn again. What made it so difficult was that many people became so savvy that it lost real connection to who they were supporting. If they saw the representatives from a certain party coming, they would rush to put on the T-shirt with that party's candidate. If they saw another, they would put on another. They had different T-shirts, and that way they could get as many goodies from as many candidates as possible. For many people this was a way of scratching a little more at their bare-bones survival and enjoying the largess that was available for such a limited time. I understood this. But it put a financial burden on all of us, because you really had to respond to these things. You could not afford to be left out."

CHAPTER 7

Flow of Information

Mark Davis

On September 8th, 2004, a few hours after CBS aired that evening's *60 Minutes II*, an Atlanta Lawyer known online as Buckhead," sat down at his keyboard. Buckhead was about to post a comment in a Free Republic forum responding to claims made in the show, setting in motion a chain of events that would once and for all destroy big media's control of the news. No longer could mainstream media outlets force-feed a docile, starving public their version of the news, and no more could public figures manage their image by managing the press. A revolution was brewing and a bogeyman of the Right, CBS Evening News anchor Dan Rather, was cast as Louis XVI.

Buckhead's Free Republic post challenged Rather's assertion on 60 Minutes that CBS had copies of authentic documents from the early 1970's purporting to prove that President George W. Bush was given favorable treatment during his Texas Air National Guard service. Buckhead claimed that "every single one of these memos to file is in a proportionally spaced font, probably Palatino or Times New Roman. In 1972 people used typewriters for this sort of thing, and typewriters used monospaced fonts." The Power Line blog subsequently joined the fray, compiling posts from readers challenging other aspects of the memos. The following day a writer from the blog Little Green Footballs typed one of the 1973 memos into Microsoft Word and found it to be an exact match. The jig was up and by January four CBS employees associated with the memo broadcast were fired and in March, Rather resigned. One of the most powerful men in media, a broadcast network news anchor, was brought down by his audience.

Similar audience uprisings had occurred before. In 1998 online news aggregator Matt Drudge broke the Monica Lewinsky story that resulted in the impeachment of President Bill Clinton. In 2002 segregationist comments made by Trent Lott were ignored by the media but distributed by bloggers, ultimately forcing Lott's resignation. The audience had slowly been wresting away from big media control of the message, but in 2004 CBS was completely unprepared not just for the rebellion of its audience, but for the speed at which it happened.

Beyond speed and control, the flow of information has also changed. Today's main sources of news and information - professional media, primary sources, and the audience - have always existed, but in the past, nearly all information reaching the public was filtered through commercial news organizations. The difference today is in the distribution. Perhaps the most famous work of citizen journalism ever, the Zapruder film, was dependent on the media for public distribution. Had that piece of video been produced today, Abraham Zapruder would have uploaded it to YouTube, embedded it in his blog, and written about his experience (with commentators noting the shots came from the Grassy Knoll). Watergate in the Internet era? DeepThroat.com would have led the charge, helped by anonymous comments on his blog posts.

Despite the incessant reporting on the demise of professional media however, it survives, and retains much of its ability to set the news agenda for the country. Professional media though, no longer includes only newspapers, TV, radio and magazines. There are now bloggers, podcasters, and even TV comedians who make money from reporting and commenting on the news. Markos Moulitsas, founder of the blog Daily Kos, is no less a part of the media than Maureen Dowd, columnist for the New York Times. Many people, sneeringly derided by journalists for their lack of an appropriate degree or experience, now earn a living from their journalist-like digital efforts.

Perhaps even more unexpectedly, we find comedians like Jon Stewart and Stephen Colbert hosting comedy shows patterned on network nightly news broadcasts, shows which are more influential than those they parody.

The rise of the Internet now allows brands, be they consumer or corporate, personal or political, to spread their own messages without being filtered by the media. The Dean campaign in 2004 and the Obama campaign in 2008, known for their innovative use of the Internet, were simply using techniques and tools that were already in use by consumer products companies, which had been creating brand web sites, newsletters, and communities for years. Just as these brands were learning how to bypass the media when reaching consumers, Dean and Obama were learning to bypass the media when reaching voters.

The news audience, too, has learned to make its own news, although that news is often filtered through the professional media. Cell phone photos of the Virginia Tech shootings and the London underground bombing were taken by individuals on the scene and distributed to the rest of us when they were uploaded to professional news web sites. Information about the Mumbai terrorist attacks and the first photo of the USAirways Hudson River jet landing, however, were broadcast to the world over Twitter, bypassing all media outlets.

For citizen journalists and primary sources such as politicians, posting news online is only the start of the news flow. If no one is aware of the post, it doesn't exist. Simply uploading a video to YouTube or posting news to a blog doesn't mean it will be seen. It's the social web that enables distribution. The web of relationships formed through Facebook, MySpace, LinkedIn, blogs, Twitter, YouTube, Flickr, Ning, Meetup, and a myriad of other similar applications power the movement of information among news consumers. Years ago friends and neighbors only met in their yards or at their children's baseball games to discuss the events of the day. Now friends, acquaintances, and strangers from around the world discuss events online through wall posts, blog comments, tweets, text messages, and email. And when news hits this network, control of the message is an illusion. Only authenticity can survive as every message is vetted for truth and spin.

But is there any real demand for news? With newspaper readership, network news viewership, and news magazine circulation all declining, an uninterested citizenry has become conventional wisdom. Looking for answers rather than anecdotes, Princeton University professor Markus Prior has studied demand for news, and come to some interesting conclusions.

While total demand for news in the U.S. is difficult, if not impossible, to measure, in his book, *Post-Broadcast Democracy*, Prior uses weekly hours per household spent watching network news and cable news as a proxy. While network news consumption has declined over the last 20 years, cable news consumption has dramatically increased. Prior discovers, though, that "fewer Americans watch more news."

No longer are people held hostage by network news at 6pm every night as the vast amount of choice brought on by the advent of cable and the Internet has made a world of both news and entertainment choices just a click away. Those who previously watched network news out of inertia, now spend their time with entertainment on cable or online.

It turns out, though, that news consumers today are more politically partisan than those of 20 years ago. It's not that Americans as a whole are more partisan, rather, news junkies are, and always have been, more partisan. This explains the popularity of political blogs that, as vehicles of opinion, are partisan by nature.

Prior further finds that "in the current high-choice media environment, whether you are a news junkie or an entertainment fan becomes a powerful determinant of your political knowledge and turnout." The more partisan Americans are those going to the polls, a fact reflected in the decreasing volatility of election results over the last 30 years. Prior's conclusion is that for a substantial segment of our population - entertainment fans - political knowledge has decreased.

Our political future seems to be in the hands of a smaller and more partisan segment of the electorate. With more citizens spending their time reading Perez Hilton instead of Politico, we're left to wonder how these Americans could ever acquire the knowledge necessary to hold our politicians accountable through the electoral process.

It's at this point we think back to Rathergate. Initially, another claim about Bush's National Guard service that amounted to beating a dead horse was ignored by most people that Wednesday night as they watched their favorite reality show. It wasn't until the social web kicked in that the broadcast became news to the general population.

Starting in a forum, continuing to blogs and comments on those blogs, the partisan news junkies spread an important story throughout the country. Entertainment fans suddenly became aware both that there were questions about Bush's service and that Kerry partisans were lying about it. The electorate was engaged and it had one more piece of information suggesting that this was an election worth its vote.

The flow of news and the process of democracy continue to change at a startling rate, but today it's the social web that drives the engagement of the electorate.

CHAPTER 8

Reaching the Loyal Base
and Other Voters

Karen A.B. Jagoda

The Loyal Base

The use of email is seen as the most effective way overall to reach voters in the loyal base, according to all consultants surveyed in 2008. Candidate web sites are seen as just about as effective as television and cable ads.

Consultants perceive direct mail, candidate and surrogate events, phone, word of mouth, and television advertisements as effective traditional means for targeting these loyal voters.

Noted differences between party preferences are seen in the use of events, television ads, and phone with these methods being more popular with those consultants working with Democrats. There is agreement across the parties on the use of Internet tools, though those working with Democrats are more inclined to find email effective.

Between 2007 and 2008, consultants showed a significant 21% jump in their interest in using email in a campaign to reach the loyal base. Also noteworthy are the slight decreases in the perceived effectiveness of online ads and blogs and an increase in the sense that candidate web sites, social nets and webcasts are effective for this group. Perhaps after a bit of experimenting with these Internet tools there has been a reality check over early enthusiasm or maybe not enough has been spent to truly test effectiveness.

Most Effective Methods for Reaching Loyal Base Consultants by Party Affiliation-Top 3 Activities				
Activities	Total	Dem	Rep	Ind
E-mail	46%	44%	38%	42%
Direct mail	38%	32%	54%	42%
Events with candidate or surrogate	37%	38%	35%	34%
Phone	29%	33%	24%	26%
Word of mouth	28%	25%	27%	21%
TV/Cable ads	26%	34%	25%	24%
Candidate web site	25%	28%	25%	29%
Social networking sites	10%	7%	10%	8%
Debates	9%	7%	8%	5%
Blogs and podcasts	8%	8%	8%	8%
Radio ads	8%	8%	10%	13%
Online video	7%	7%	6%	13%
Online ads	5%	5%	8%	5%
Webcasts	4%	4%	6%	13%
Text messaging	4%	6%	2%	3%
Newspaper ads	4%	4%	5%	3%
Yard signs/ outdoor billboards	3%	4%	5%	3%

E-Voter Institute 2008 Seventh Annual Survey of Political and Advocacy Communications Leaders

Most Effective Methods for Reaching Loyal Base		
Historical View		
Total Consultants-Top 3 Activities		
Activities	**2007**	**2008**
E-mail	38%	46%
Direct mail	41%	38%
Events with candidate or surrogate	37%	37%
Phone	21%	29%
Word of mouth	27%	28%
TV/Cable ads	28%	26%
Candidate web site	23%	25%
Social networking sites	9%	10%
Debates	13%	9%
Radio ads	11%	8%
Blogs and podcasts	12%	8%
Online video	7%	7%
Online ads	7%	5%
Newspaper ads	6%	4%
Webcasts	3%	4%
Text messaging	2%	4%
Yard signs/ outdoor billboards	8%	3%

E-Voter Institute 2008 Seventh Annual Survey of Political and Advocacy Communications Leaders

Reaching Swing, Independent and Undecided Voters

Less than 25% of the consultants think candidate web sites and email are effective for reaching swing, Independent and undecided voters. This is, however, a 57% increase over interest expressed in 2007.

Television ads, direct mail, debates, word of mouth and candidate events are seen as the best ways to reach swing, Independent and undecided voters.

The historical view of reaching swing, Independent and undecided voters shows a 38% jump in the number of consultants thinking that online ads are effective with this group. Events with candidates and surrogates shows a noticeable increase though television and cable ads, direct mail and debates are still seen as the strongest tools for reaching these unpredictable voters.

Most Effective Methods for Reaching Swing, Independent and Undecided Voters Consultants by Party Affiliation-Top 3 Activities			
Activities	**Total**	**Dem**	**Rep**	**Ind**
TV/Cable ads	52%	60%	48%	61%
Direct mail	37%	37%	48%	50%
Debates	31%	35%	29%	24%
Word of mouth	29%	26%	29%	26%
Events with candidate or surrogate	28%	26%	24%	26%
Candidate web site	22%	17%	21%	13%
Radio ads	16%	17%	24%	29%
Phone	16%	20%	13%	11%
E-mail	13%	12%	10%	8%
Online ads	11%	13%	8%	5%
Online video	11%	8%	13%	13%
Social networking sites	11%	7%	8%	5%
Newspaper ads	5%	4%	6%	5%
Yard signs/outdoor billboards	4%	6%	3%	5%
Blogs and podcasts	4%	4%	6%	5%
Webcasts	3%	0%	6%	8%
Text messaging	1%	0%	2%	3%

E-Voter Institute 2008 Seventh Annual Survey of Political and Advocacy Communications Leaders

Most Effective Methods for Reaching Swing, Independent, Undecided Voters Historic View		
Consultants 2007-2008 Top 3 Activities		
Activities	2007	2008
TV/Cable ads	48%	52%
Direct mail	36%	37%
Debates	34%	31%
Word of mouth	30%	29%
Events with candidate or surrogate	25%	28%
Candidate web site	14%	22%
Radio ads	20%	16%
Phone	15%	16%
E-mail	11%	13%
Online ads	8%	11%
Online video	11%	11%
Social networking sites	8%	11%
Newspaper ads	7%	5%
Yard signs/outdoor billboards	10%	4%
Blogs and podcasts	9%	4%
Webcasts	3%	3%
Text messaging	2%	1%

E-Voter Institute 2008 Seventh Annual Survey of Political and Advocacy Communications Leaders

CHAPTER 9

Three's Company:
Unscripted Politics, Humor
and the Unofficial Campaign

Larry Ward

It's easy to think of politics as theatre, with verbose figures filled with passion, vocalizing a common vision for their audience. Our imagination overflows with romanticized images of pleated suits, sharp wits and silver tongues. Today, nearly everything in politics is calculated, where votes are pre-tabulated and speeches are scripted. However, there are certain instances, when politics is not a Broadway show but an improvisational cabaret. While this piece could be dedicated solely to political missteps of the last election cycle, I will try to focus on three areas: unscripted politics, humor and the unofficial campaign.

Some of our country's greatest refrains and biggest gaffes are borne out of nowhere. Most notably might be Ronald Reagan's impromptu decision (against the will of advisors) to include "Mr. Gorbachev, tear down this wall" in his 1981 speech from the Brandenberg Gate of West Berlin, Germany.

Politics is often a war of words. Battle lines are drawn, where candidates are revered by supporters and reviled by their opposition. These skirmishes are won by defining your opponent and creating a resonating message with voters. But in some cases, worse than any attack ad, a single verbal blunder can be a campaign's own worst enemy. Moreover, the 2008 election gave us enough bipartisan fodder akin to a reality television show. Both candidates and their running mates had their fair share of political bloopers.

One need not look any further than Joe Biden. In September 2008, roughly eight weeks from the general election, the vice-presidential candidate was at a campaign rally in Missouri. While recognizing Missouri Democrat, Chuck Graham in the audience, Biden told the State Senator, "Chuck, stand up, let 'em see you." What he didn't realize is that Chuck Graham is a paraplegic, confined to a wheelchair. Take another example, then-candidate Barack Obama, in a speech in Oregon. During one point in the speech Obama stated, "Over the last fifteen months, we've traveled to every corner of the United States. I've now been in 57 states, I think — one left to go."

If you think these laughable liberals are the only political missteps, then perhaps you've forgotten some of the gaffes of the GOP. Senator John McCain, when asked by a voter if he would "send an airmail message to Tehran," insinuating decisive military action against Iran. McCain candidly joked about an old Beach Boys song, in a raspy tone, "Bomb bomb bomb, bomb bomb, Iran."

But still some of the most talked about events came at the expense of Republican vice presidential candidate Sarah Palin. The infamous line, "I can see Russia from my house," incites laughter to any Saturday Night Live follower. Despite the strong physical characteristics between Palin and her impressionist Tina Fey, the important thing to note is that she never actually said that! So in the age of You Tube, Facebook and Twitter, we witnessed every single one of these blunders exploited by their opposition, inflicting as much damage as possible.

Having said that lends a perfect segue into our next topic: humor. Mark Twain once wrote, "Humor is mankind's greatest blessing."

Americans spend hours every day watching sitcoms, forwarding cartoons and indulging in watching funny pictures, gut-busting stories and uproarious viral videos. A Beltway truism holds that politics makes strange bedfellows. As such, humor and politics might be the epitome of an "odd couple." Humor is often the "girl next door" in the litany of politics' bunk-mates. Humor, like the girl next door, is magnificent, and yet often largely under-appreciated.

When used effectively, humor can be looked at as the prom queen. Jokes are often quick punch lines used in political stump speeches. But more recently, we've seen humor taking a bigger role in the political arena. As President of Political Media, Inc, I've seen a shift in the way we've become creatures of new habits. We're constantly looking for a quick fix. In the clutter of email inboxes these days, we receive inspirational prayers with angels forwarded from our mothers, we ignore long emails, and forward the funny, angry and the thought provoking ones to coworkers, friends and relatives.

In 2006, Political Media Inc. was given the unique opportunity to work with nine states with ballot initiatives dealing with Eminent Domain. The challenges were immense. In any good issue-advocacy campaign, we had to educate the general public first, and then attempt to persuade. To be honest, Eminent Domain isn't what you would call a "hot button" political issue. Abortion, gun-rights, stem-cell research, affirmative action, death penalty, gay marriage-- these are what people remember, and evoke strong emotions from both sides.

So how does one go about educating a relatively uninformed general public, while attempting to persuade a less-than captive audience? Even if we were successful educating, it wouldn't guarantee that they will be persuaded on the issue, much less motivated enough to show up to the polls on Election Day. Given this set of unique challenges, we decided to create a web-animated parody. We produced a three and a half minute animation as a spoof of the HBO Series "The Sopranos." The skit depicted elected officials running a mob-style government; in order to evict property owners for the benefit of the mafia led "Bada-Bing Development Corporation." Political Media customized the animation for each state, based on issue and locality, and launched it weeks prior to Election Day.

Prior to launch, Political Media led an informal focus group. The focus group did not understand the Eminent Domain issue. In fact, 20 out of 24 likely voters had not even heard the term "Eminent Domain." After we played the animation for the group, they understood the issue and became passionate about preventing Eminent Domain abuse. On Election Day, we were successful in nearly every single state with statewide ballot initiatives.

Typically, we hear about a campaign's decision to "go negative." Candidates, staffers and consultants, all contemplate the strategy, of when, how and in what way. Simply put, going negative works, and going negative wins campaigns. It's a highly effective strategy that defines the race on your terms.

For our Eminent Domain campaigns however, we needed a better message to tell people to oppose the issue. To really think outside the box, we had to challenge conventional wisdom. We knew we wouldn't be as successful by simply going negative. Instead we decided to "go goofy." As an F.B.I. (Fully Blooded Italian), I envisioned a cartoon Tony

Soprano and his tough talking Mafioso group. This bold look caught like wildfire- spreading all over the Internet, and filling inboxes in states we had not even placed the animation! The important lesson I learned was in order to be funny, we had to have a clear and consistent message.

From candid politicians to the idea of going negative by going goofy, we often see politics take a life-form all its own. It's assumed in the marketing of any campaign that third party testimonials offer tremendous amounts of credibility. But what happens when a third party is not a facet of the campaign? You get You Tube songs like "I got a crush on Obama" from Barely Political. In the 3 minute 25 second video, the smitten singer, better known as Obama-Girl sings: (put in the link to the video? Yes.)www.youtube.com/watch?v=wKsoXHYICqU

You're into border security
Let's break this border between you and me
Universal healthcare reform
It makes me warm… cuz I got a crush on Obama.

We've seen many forms of the unofficial campaign. For example, the Ron Paul "Revolution.":www.time.com/time/politics/article/0,8599,1678661,00.html

Although, not an official arm of the Ron Paul campaign, the "revolution," became a staple in his campaign. Proponents of limited government, constitutionalism and non-interventionalism became de facto ambassadors for the Ron Paul brand later dubbed "Pauliens." Despite an unsuccessful bid for the GOP nomination, the fundraising and support base he garnered, under such limited resources will be the measuring stick for years to come. But third parties don't always show up in droves. Sometimes all it takes is one match to ignite a firestorm.

While at CPAC www.cpac.org/ (Conservative Political Action) this year, we tried to find a way to break through the clutter of handouts given to attendees and exhibitors alike. We needed something current and eye-catching, yet unmistakable. This is how we came up with one of the conference's hottest items: the "Obama Stimulus Dollar." With Political Media's logo, contact information and ad hoc site (printfunnymoney. com) printed on the back; the front side featured a convincingly fake dollar bill. With a "Left" leaning portrait of Obama, underneath scrolled the word "Change." The stimulus dollar also featured a treasury seal with the words "Department of Obamunism."

At the top of the bill, read the words, "United Nations Note" with the phrase "In Gov We Trust" and "The Socialist State of America" on either side of Obama. Towards the bottom of the dollar read: "This note is illegal tender for all debts, foreclosures & bailouts." It was a great piece of marketing for us, because everyone wanted to read it.

Who can forget the "Hillary 1984" ad? The spin off of Apple's "1984" ad, created by an "anonymous" YouTube user began the "Change" theme of the 2008 campaign. Unofficial campaigns like this can take off like a runaway train.

It's worth mentioning (and goes without saying) that in the 24/7 cable news cycle and You Tube era, campaigns and candidates must always be on. Over the last few years nothing has grown faster than viral video. A fast moving viral ad can get more eyeballs than prime time television... and for a lot less. Viral marketing does not happen by accident or happenstance. Viral marketing requires as much thought and preparation as any other media buy.

It's important to understand the elements that make viral videos light the Internet on fire. Political Media strives to incorporate humor, but also anger or sentiment into our productions. While we take great comfort in the exaggerated, slap-stick, sarcastic, self-deprecating and generally funny moments in our life, it's quite difficult to translate that into driving a message.

Humor, once looked at as a distraction for serious, political discourse, has been overtaken by cable networks. Cable television has transformed the way we get our news. No longer are we confined between the dinner time hours for news.

We now see an incredible shift from political news to political commentary. Walter Cronkite and Peter Jennings have been replaced by comedian-political-commentators, John Stewart and Steven Colbert on the left and Dennis Miller on the right.

Politics is ever-present and ever changing. Stay on top, stick wit it, or go sleep wit da fishes... Tony Soprano's orders.

E-Voter Institute on Unofficial Campaigns

The rise of the unofficial campaign is fueled by the growing ability of voters to post comments on blogs and other sites about a wide variety of interests. According to E-Voter Institute 2008 post election survey of voters, posting to blogs rose from 28-31% between May and November and posting ratings or comments increased from 46-51% with the biggest jump—7%—in those 25-34 years old and those 65-74 years old. One-third of those who voted at the poll post to blogs while only 19% of those who did not vote did so.

General Internet Use (by those who did/did not vote in 2008 election)				
Online Activities	Total	Voted at the poll	Voted absentee/ mail-in	Did not vote
Use email	94%	94%	95%	92%
Make online purchases	80%	81%	84%	66%
Forward links and email to friends/family	73%	74%	75%	64%
Read newspapers or magazines online	66%	68%	68%	51%
Play online games	56%	56%	53%	58%
Download video and/or audio	53%	54%	55%	46%
Post ratings or comments online	51%	52%	53%	36%
Social network member	49%	50%	47%	47%
Listen to online radio	45%	46%	48%	37%
Upload video and/or audio	32%	33%	32%	24%
Post to other blogs	31%	33%	28%	19%
Maintain a blog or your own web site	23%	24%	23%	17%
Use widgets	21%	21%	23%	16%
Subscribe to RSS feeds	20%	21%	22%	12%
Twitter, other micro blogs	9%	9%	11%	4%

E-Voter Institute 2008 Post Election Survey of Voter Expectations

CHAPTER 10

Breaking Through the Media Clutter

Karen A.B. Jagoda

Traditional media are still the most popular news sources for voters.

According to the E-Voter Institute 2008 Survey of Voter Expectations, Democrats are more likely to get their news from newspapers, and network and local television, while Republicans are more likely to get news from local television, newspapers, and cable news. Independents tend to rely on local television, newspapers and web sites as their top news sources. In general, cable news is just about equal to web sites as a trusted news source for all voters.

What follows are results on how voters get their news and what they consider the best ways to get their attention about candidates and issues. Differences between party affiliation, age and geographic location are all illustrated and there are surprising similarities as well as stark differences.

These results confirm suspicions and other research data about news-gathering habits and raises issues about how to reach the audience that is not tuning into traditional media.

Voters' Most Relied Upon News Sources By Political Affiliation -Among Top 3

News Sources	Dem	Rep	Ind
Local television	47%	45%	45%
Newspapers	46%	43%	44%
Network television	40%	36%	37%
Cable news	36%	38%	36%
Web sites	34%	34%	39%
Friends and family	19%	21%	20%
Radio	17%	24%	19%
Debates	13%	12%	12%
Candidate commercials	10%	8%	7%
Search engine	8%	9%	8%
E-mail	8%	9%	8%
Magazines	7%	5%	8%
Blogs	5%	5%	6%
People from work	5%	6%	5%
Online social networks	4%	4%	4%
Books	1%	2%	1%

E-Voter Institute 2008 Third Annual Survey of Voter Expectations

News Sources	18-24	25-34	35-54	55-64	65-74	75+
Voters' Most Relied Upon News Sources						
By Age-Among Top 3						
Newspapers	36%	38%	47%	53%	59%	61%
television	26%	31%	39%	49%	50%	61%
Local television	33%	41%	49%	52%	54%	46%
E-mail	8%	9%	8%	8%	8%	7%
Cable news	33%	32%	37%	41%	40%	32%
commercials	6%	7%	9%	11%	13%	7%
Search engine	10%	12%	7%	5%	3%	4%
networks	8%	6%	3%	1%	2%	0%
Radio	14%	19%	20%	21%	18%	43%
family	28%	26%	18%	13%	11%	7%
Web sites	51%	42%	32%	26%	16%	7%
Debates	11%	11%	13%	12%	14%	18%
Magazines	12%	8%	5%	5%	5%	7%
Blogs	13%	7%	4%	2%	3%	0%
Books	2%	2%	1%	0%	1%	0%
People from work	7%	9%	4%	1%	0%	0%

E-Voter Institute 2008 Third Annual Survey of Voter Expectations

Previous E-Voter Institute surveys of voters provides an historical view of the most trusted news sources. This research shows that local television has overtaken newspapers as one of the top two sources of information. Network television seems to be gaining in favor along with cable news. Voters also seem to be showing less interest in radio, email, and magazines and strong, though slightly less interest in web sites.

News Sources	2006 Voters	2007 Voters	2008 Voters
Local television	54%	41%	46%
Newspapers	59%	45%	45%
Network television	47%	29%	38%
Cable news	20%	34%	36%
Web sites	37%	37%	35%
Friends and family	18%	23%	20%
Radio	18%	28%	19%
Debates	N/A	N/A	12%
Candidate commercials	10%	8%	9%
E-mail	13%	11%	8%
Search engine	8%	8%	8%
Magazines	7%	11%	7%
Blogs	4%	7%	6%
People from work	5%	6%	5%
Online social networks	N/A	6%	4%
Books	1%	3%	1%

Voters' Most Relied Upon News Sources Historical View-Among Top 3

E-Voter Institute 2008 Third Annual Survey of Voter Expectations

In the post election 2008 E-Voter Institute survey, nearly half the people everywhere seem to share an interest in local newspaper sites, while urban dwellers are much more likely to use national newspaper sites to find news and information. Significantly fewer people in rural areas are interested in sports sites, entertainment and fashion sites, and search engines than those in other areas.

Suburban and exurban people are the most likely to use cable news with 39% reporting so. Likewise, 39% of those same people use news related web sites to find out about current events.

Voters' Most Relied Upon News Sources By Geographic Location-Among Top 3			
News Sources	Rural	Urban	Sub/Ex Urban
Newspapers	35%	37%	34%
Network television	38%	35%	35%
Local television	46%	38%	41%
E-mail	10%	8%	7%
Cable news	35%	35%	39%
Candidate commercials	3%	2%	3%
Search engines	8%	9%	7%
Online social networks	5%	5%	4%
Radio	18%	19%	21%
Friends and family	22%	20%	20%
News related web sites	34%	37%	39%
General interest web sites	8%	8%	10%
Large portal sites	17%	16%	16%
Debates	7%	7%	8%
Magazines	5%	7%	5%
Blogs	4%	9%	6%
Books	1%	1%	1%
People from work	3%	4%	4%

E-Voter Institute 2008 Post Election Survey of Voters

Social Network Members

In the 2008 E-Voter Institute research, a nearly equal number of active social network members (63%) say that television and cable ads are as effective as the official candidate web site (62%) to get their attention. The most active social net members tend to use traditional media significantly less than the average voter.

Close behind are debates for this active group of social networkers. For non-members of a social net, television ads and debates are seen as effective by at least half and 45% say the official web site gets their attention.

Online ads are seen as more effective than newspaper ads by active social net members. Every category of activity is higher for social net members than non-members, suggesting perhaps that social net members are more curious in general and interested in news and what others are saying. Active social net members show the highest interest in text messaging, far more than the average voter.

Best Ways to Get Voters' Attention (by social network status)				
Activities	Total Voters	Member updates often	Member updates not often	Non Member
Television/cable ads	63%	63%	64%	62%
Debates	57%	60%	62%	53%
Official web site	51%	62%	58%	45%
Word of mouth	39%	49%	47%	33%
Direct mail	31%	34%	30%	31%
Newspaper ads	29%	31%	28%	30%
Radio ads	26%	27%	27%	25%
Online ads	25%	35%	27%	21%
E-mail from candidate or celebrity endorser	22%	33%	23%	19%
Webcasts	20%	30%	24%	15%
Yard signs, outdoor billboards	20%	26%	21%	17%
Independent blog posting	16%	30%	20%	10%
Social networking sites	15%	36%	20%	7%
Viral video about a candidate	14%	28%	18%	9%
Phone	9%	15%	7%	8%
Text messaging	5%	11%	3%	4%

E-Voter Institute 2008 Third Annual Survey of Voter Expectations

These active social networkers use the Internet significantly more than those who are not members of any social net.

- Active social net members are twice as likely to use blogs as a news source than non-members.
- All social net members are over 40% more likely to use web sites for news than non-members.
- Active social net members are 27% less likely to use local television than non-members to find out about news.
- Less than one in ten active social net members rely on social nets for news.

Voters' Most Relied Upon News Sources

By Social Network Status

News Sources	Total Voters	Member updates often	Member updates not often	Non Member
Local television	46%	36%	45%	49%
Newspapers	45%	39%	40%	48%
Network television	38%	32%	36%	40%
Cable news	36%	35%	35%	36%
Web sites	35%	43%	42%	30%
Friends and family	20%	21%	23%	19%
Radio	19%	16%	19%	20%
Debates	12%	14%	12%	12%
Candidate commercials	9%	10%	8%	8%
Search engine	8%	10%	8%	8%
E-mail	8%	11%	8%	8%
Magazines	7%	7%	6%	7%
Blogs	6%	8%	7%	4%
People from work	5%	5%	5%	5%
Online social networks	4%	10%	4%	2%
Books	1%	2%	0%	1%

E-Voter Institute 2008 Third Annual Survey of Voter Expectations

PART III
The Campaign

CHAPTER 11

Webolution

T.A. Berg

Many political observers credit the Internet for the success of Barrack Obama's campaign – particularly in the 2008 Presidential primary. It's overly simplistic to say that the internet alone was responsible for winning an US Presidential campaign, but it's clear that social networks, internet messaging and video and online contributions played a major role in electing America's 44th President.

Pundits are abuzz either predicting or decrying the power of the Internet in the modern political campaign and the impact on democracy. But looking at the evolution of other mediums in political communication and the real role of the internet in effective campaigns, we can see that the internet doesn't replace any particular mode of communication, however, it displaces some as it elbows its way into the pantheon of communication, organizing and fundraising tools.

In the 1960 election, TV had been around for a while, but had not yet played a decisive role in political campaigns. But that year, the emotional issues driving at the time matched the visual power of TV; John F Kennedy was a young, telegenic candidate who's strengths conveyed well on TV, and improvements in technology and programming to attract viewers that made commercials and televised debates critical, all combined to launch TV into the mainstream of the political ethos of the US.

All new forms of communication go through erratic growth as the social landscape shifts and technology changes. The medium evolves to match the issues/political environment; the technology and content must also evolve to attract a sufficient audience, and the campaign needs must fit with the context of the medium to generate sufficient energy.

Much like TV in the 1960's, the Internet is starting to come of age – propelled in part by the right candidate, right conditions and right time to move the medium forward. Like TV, which did not simply replace broadsheets and other forms of communication, the Internet is not replacing TV as the primary medium of our political conversation. Instead, it is creating a more fundamental change as it adds to the mix of political communication methods and how those mediums interact with each other.

The first use of the Internet, digital communication over telephone lines, was primarily a tool for sharing data between academic and scientific institutions. But that changed with the advent of the personal computer and companies saw a commercial application for the technology. In 1985 Control Video Corporation (CVC) saw the Internet as a tool for selling Atari game updates. CVC evolved into America Online in 1989 – which launched an aggressive marketing campaign to popularize online communication in the form of web content and email to compete with Compuserve (another pioneer online service that was used extensively by the technical community). And by 1992, millions of the now iconic free AOL CD's were flowing to mailboxes.

That same year the earliest campaign websites appeared almost as an after-thought; one of those things you roll out just to say that you had. US Senators Diane Feinstein and Ted Kennedy were among the first politicians to put up websites that were little more than an online biography. Prior to the 1992 Presidential campaign, President H. W. Bush looked to be cruising to re-election; a little-known Arkansas Governor, Bill Clinton, looked to be just another also-ran vying to face Bush who was overshadowed by national heavy-weights like Virginia Governor Douglas Wilder, Nebraska Senator Bob Kerry and former California Governor Jerry Brown.

In a campaign struggling to get any traction, Clinton's Internet Director, Jock Gill, became one of the first political operatives to see the net as a potential organizing tool – primarily to get information directly to activists and supporters – because the mainstream media largely ignored their campaign in the early months. After Bush stumbled into a recession and seemed detached from the struggles of regular voters, Clinton won in a fairly decisive election using mostly traditional media to deliver his message (it's the economy stupid). He did, however, become the first Presidential candidate to include the Internet in his regular stump speeches and campaign platform – promising to use the web to make government more accessible to the public. Every candidate since then has talked about the value of the Internet to empower the public, improve efficiency and expand access.

By the 1996 campaign, the Internet was widely used as an alternative communication method in nearly every large campaign. Although the Internet had arrived on the national campaign scene, no one really understood exactly how to use it – but at least it was no longer relegated to the kids' table. Every election cycle since then has witnessed an exponential expansion in the use of online campaigning. Since then, there has also been a recognition that the freewheeling nature of the internet could not be controlled – it would magnify mistakes and misinformation, decentralize news, and give anyone with an internet connection the power to impact elections or public policy.

1996 also marked the start of what would eventually be called the "blogosphere," with broadcast emails from Matt Drudge called "the Report" – a gossipy look at politics. (www.drudgereport.com/) The

"Drudge Report" began offering an alternative to traditional media and got a huge boost when it beat the mainstream media in breaking the Monica Lewinsky story. Drudge, along with other blogs like the FlashReport, began as email links to traditional media sources, but have since evolved to include a lot of original commentary and news. This new variation of the Internet would have a dramatic impact on the body politic –wresting the power of information control away from traditional media, government and campaigns.

In 1998, a professional wrestler, body builder and showman from Minnesota ran as a third party candidate against Democrat AG Hubert Humphrey III and Republican Mayor of St. Paul, Norm Coleman (later a US Senator who was defeated in 2008 by comedian Al Franken). Jess Ventura's campaign was not taken seriously by the mainstream media, power brokers or donors – so he turned to the Internet to deliver his message. In a quirky election where the main candidates battered each other and voters were allowed to register and vote at the same moment, Ventura was the right kind of candidate to tap into angry voters using the Internet – organizing and directing a hostile public to the voting booth to support change in the form of an inexperienced Governor.

By the 2000 Presidential campaign, the Internet had become the latest buzz – everyone was touting their plan as the next big thing. But the Internet remained a secondary medium, with the vast majority of campaign dollars, brainpower and strategy still focused on traditional paid and earned media. While you had to be on the web to be a "real candidate," no had yet figured out how to use the Internet as a powerful campaign tool. At the same time, commercial use of the Internet was exploding – Ebay was launched, AOL had millions of subscribers, Microsoft was battling to lure away those AOL subscribers, Google began selling search ads and the investment community was focused on e-commerce. Most of the tools of the modern Internet campaign were now in place.

2002 marked the birth of *social* networking sites like Friendster and MySpace. The Internet had established itself as a tool for communicating with supporters who were already dedicated to the candidate. The Internet had also worked its way into the lexicon of campaigning – every candidate talked about the future, and the internet was the ubiquitous example of the future of commerce, communication and citizen empowerment. That year web sites began to emerge as legitimate alternatives to the mainstream media – and the big news organizations were scrambling to get on board.

By 2004 the Internet's power for organizing and mobilizing supporters had already been seen. It had evolved to the point where it was core campaign function: every Presidential campaign (and nearly every major campaign across the nation) – had an "e-team." But campaigns were still searching to find the right use of the Internet.

While Clinton and Ventura were two of the first large campaigns to successfully use the Internet as a campaign tool, Democrat Howard Dean from Vermont was among the first truly "wired" candidates. The Internet was a central component of his campaign. Much has been written about Dean's online fundraising and that certainly was a major factor in propelling him from obscurity to front-runner; but perhaps more importantly was Dean's use of the Internet to reach out to and mobilize young people and liberals who felt ignored by the mainstream candidates. He interacted with activists through the Internet, he read blogs – he molded his message and campaign based on input from the online community. Nearly 150,000 supporters had found each other through Meetup.com and were busy organizing to help in early caucus and primary states.

His meltdown was also fueled by the Internet – his early successes led to an embrace of political insiders to the dismay of his insurgent "wired supporters" and the millions of subsequent "did you see this" emails and videos chronicling Dean's over-the-top response after losing the Iowa caucuses largely ended his campaign. But the lessons were not lost on the other candidates – John Edwards shifted his campaign strategy to focus on Internet town hall meetings to appeal to Dean's wired supporters.

In 2005, YouTube was launched, giving activists and candidates another tool – self-generated content and a platform for distributing it. Today, millions of videos are speeding through digital lines with messages from nearly every campaign from school board to President. Facebook – which had gone online the year before – already had over a million subscribers in 2006. Every year, new tools came online that made it easier.

In 2008 the internet had arrived center stage: according to a study by the Pew Internet and American Life Project, over 70 percent of voters got at least some of their political information from the Internet. Major candidates used YouTube, Facebook or Twitter to launch their campaigns; most campaigns utilized search ads, pop-up banners, and personal blogs; nearly everyone collected user data; and user-driven content and organization was prevalent.

The impact of the Internet on campaigns, politics, and public policy has been more evolutionary than revolutionary; but there is no denying the Internet is changing the way campaigns – large and small – are run today. The evolution has been a lurching progress – and, it's accelerating as technologies align, costs drop and professionals better understand effective uses of the Internet.

A recent study by the Pew Institute showed that 46 percent of voters received at least some of their political information from the Internet – although a host of surveys indicate that this is far more focused on candidates who already enjoy a high profile/awareness.

During the 2008 Presidential election, GOP candidate John McCain collected more than 600,000 Facebook "friends," and half of Obama's donors contributed online. Joseph Anthony, a non-political Californian, created a Facebook group supporting Senator Barrack Obama, collected more than 200,000 supporters. At the same time, more than 60% of voters say that Internet is full of misinformation.

From the earliest candidate websites that were little more than electronic brochures, less than ten years passed before all the tools were available for the multi-faceted Internet campaigns we see today – and most experts agree the phenomenon will only expand.

Barriers still exist: niche companies tout unrealistic and expensive technology, the power and limits of the Internet are not fully understood, spoofs and hoaxes have left the public suspicious, and it still mostly speaks to those who are already politically involved – not the mass of undecided less interested voters.

But campaigns at every level must incorporate Internet strategies – strategies plural, because throwing out a website that is little more than an electronic brochure simply won't cut it in today's wired world.

CHAPTER 12

Calls vs. Clicks: Examining Web and Telephone Polls in the 2008 Election

Christopher P. Borick

In some ways it's like a death watch. Every election cycle pollsters across America hold their collective breath and wait and see if their major means of gauging voter preferences has survived another election cycle. For years, the vital signs of telephone based surveys in the United States have been headed downwards. Plummeting response rates and decreasing population coverage have led many in the public opinion research field to speculate that standard random digit dialing (RDD) surveys were headed to the graveyard. During the 2008 campaign anticipation was high not only for the actual outcome of the races, but also for the performance of the hundreds of polls that attempted to predict the results. In this article I examine if the elections of 2008 marked the end for the classic telephone poll in American elections and look at the performance of web based surveys as a replacement for the RDD method.

The long awaited demise of the telephone-based election poll seemed to have arrived in early February of 2008 when the polls proved to be far off the final results of the Democratic Party primary election in New

Hampshire. According to a Pollster.com (2008) average of the last 5 polls before the primary, Barack Obama was beating Hillary Clinton by over 7 percentage points. However, when the votes were counted on election night, Clinton beat Obama by 3 percent (39% to 36%). The poor performance in New Hampshire followed fairly poor polling during the Iowa Caucus, thus adding to the chorus that the end of the telephone poll had finally happened. But as it appeared the RDD polls were down for the count, they made a triumphant return as primary season progressed through the spring of 2008 and into the general election in the fall.

On average, the polls in 2008 were very accurate in predicting the results of the presidential election and most statewide races. According to the National Council on Public Polls (NCPP) the polls during the last election were as accurate as they were in 2004 and projected the actual outcome quite accurately.

Every national poll showed Barack Obama winning the race, with the average margin of victory for the Democratic nominee measuring 7.5 percentage points. The actual margin of victory for Obama over John McCain was 6.8 percent. The results at the state level were also quite solid, with state polls averaging less than 2 points off the final results. (National Council on Public Polls, 2008). Importantly, the accuracy of these state polls in 2008 was about the same as it was in elections throughout the decade. This stability in accuracy came despite the vaunted threats from declining response rates and cell phone only households.

TABLE ONE
Candidate Error in State Polls: 2002 -2008

YEAR	NUMBER OF POLLS	CANDIDATE ERROR
2002	98	2.30%
2004	198	1.70%
2006	152	2.00%
2008	236	1.80%

If the standard telephone polls had a good year in 2008, the results for Internet based surveys were very mixed. One of the biggest users of Internet based surveys, Zogby International, had limited success in predicting election outcomes.

The well regarded web site, fivethirtyeight.com, conducted an analysis of Zogby Internet surveys. The analysis shows Zogby's statewide surveys missed Obama's vote percentage by an average of 5.4%, and incorrectly picked the winner in 3 of the 11 states he polled.

Comparatively, the average miss for Obama's vote percentage in all statewide polls was only about 2.5%. Some of Zogby's misses were notably off, with the polling firm showing John McCain winning Ohio by almost five points and Obama actually winning the state by over 4 points.

TABLE TWO

State	Zogby	Actual Result	Difference
NV	Obama +0.4%	Obama +12.5%	12.1
OH	McCain +4.7%	Obama +4.5%	9.2
CO	Obama +1.0%	Obama +9.0%	8
NM	Obama +7.8%	Obama +15.1%	7.3
MO	Obama +5.7%	McCain +0.1%	5.8
IN	McCain +4.2%	Obama +1.0%	5.2
NH	Obama + 5.1%	Obama +9.6%	4.5
NC	Obama + 3.4%	Obama +0.3%	3.1
FL	Obama + 1.1%	Obama +2.8%	1.7
VA	Obama + 7.8%	Obama +6.3%	1.5
PA	Obama + 11.4%	Obama +10.3%	0.9

Source: fivethirtyeight.com

While Zogby International's Internet surveys did not perform well in 2008, Harris Interactive's election efforts proved fairly successful. Harris Interactive's final presidential election poll was fairly accurate in predicting the final national numbers.

The Harris Internet poll showed Obama beating McCain 52% to 44%, not far off from the actual 53% to 46% election results. Harris used a very large sample (5,210) to make its projection, with its demographic splits matching up very closely with exit poll results (See Table Three)

TABLE THREE

	Harris Interactive Obama Results	Exit Poll Obama Results
Male	50%	49%
Female	53%	56%
Bush Voters 2004	15%	18%
Kerry Voters 2004	87%	89%
Republicans	11%	9%
Democrats	87%	89%
Independents	51%	52%
East	59%	59%
Midwest	50%	54%
South	47%	46%
West	53%	55%

Harris Interactive Results in Comparison to Exit Polls
Harris Interactive: 2008

The variability in the predictive ability of the Zogby and Harris Interactive results may be the product of factors such as sample size, however, it is more likely that the sample selection methods for these surveys is behind the varied accuracy of the polls. The primary problem with Internet polls is the wide variability in sampling.

Unlike the standardized nature of telephone polls, Internet sampling is often both unspecified by the polling firm and prone to self selection effects. As Charles Franklin wrote, "It is reasonable that the people who volunteer to take political polls on the Internet are considerably more interested in politics and likely more strongly partisan than is a random sample of likely voters."(Franklin, 2007) Thus the makeup of Internet samples plagues the reliability of web polls and leads to the widely varied accuracy that can be seen between the Zogby and Harris Interactive efforts in 2008.

With telephone polls being compromised by declining response rates and coverage issues, and web-based surveys plagued by sampling problems, it appears that the future of election polling is in jeopardy. Ironically, it may be the merging of both of these technologies that represents the future of election polling in the United States.

The prime example of the confluence of phone and Internet surveys is the work of the Knowledge Networks with their cutting edge methodology of public opinion polling. The inability of Internet surveys to produce probability-based results has plagued the predictive ability of surveys on the web.

Among academic researchers, Knowledge Networks has the only online data set that could be used to produce probability-based results. Others like Zogby and Harris really can't claim a probability basis and thus can't claim margin of error for their polls. It's not that online polls can't be good; it's just that they are not based on probability functions. Knowledge Networks is really the model that is bridging the gap between the era of the phone survey and web surveys. Others will follow but right now they are the gold standard.

Knowledge Networks has built an online panel through the use of telephone based recruiting. Through random sampling of landline telephone households with both listed and unlisted numbers, Knowledge Networks developed a nationally representative sample of voters. In order to ensure that all of the individuals in the panel have Internet access, Knowledge Networks provides Internet access to all households that did not have web based access. The combination of probability based phone recruitment and full Internet access allows this company to conduct online surveys that are nationally representative.

In the 2008 presidential campaign Knowledge Networks teamed with the Associated Press and Yahoo to conduct a series of election polls through their Internet panel. The results of their final poll released a few days before the presidential election had Obama beating McCain by an 8 point margin (51% to 43%). This poll also tracked very closely with telephone polls throughout the election season, and along with Knowledge Networks' other research has established the hybrid telephone-Internet methodology as an emerging standard for election polls.

As the book is closed on the 2008 polling season it appears that the eulogies for the telephone poll were premature. Through the gauntlet of cell phone only households and caller-ID induced declines in response, the RDD poll once again performed quite well.

While there were clearly failures such as the New Hampshire primary, the overall performance of the telephone polls in 2008 was strong and equal in accuracy to polls from early elections during the decade. And as the telephone polls generally hit the mark during the 2008 campaign, their Internet counterparts turned out to run hot and cold.

The emergence of the hybrid telephone-Internet survey methodology from Knowledge Networks has helped usher in the arrival of web surveys to the big leagues, but the opt-in world of Internet polls has yet to emerge as the replacement or even equal to the old standby. Thus the death-watch will go on until at least the mid-terms of 2010.

REFERENCES

American Association of Public Opinion Research. 2009. *An Evaluation of the Methodology of the 2008 Pre-Election Primary Polls*. (March,2009).www.aapor.org/uploads/AAPOR_Press_Releases/AAPOR_Rept_of_the_ad_hoc_committee.pdf

Fram, Alan and Trevor Thompson, (2008). "AP poll shows Obama backers gleeful, McCain's Glum," *Yahoo News*, (November,1)news.yahoo.com/page/election-2008-political-pulse;_ylt=AqupBy.vrq2htRu0SdRDWN3LUpF4

Franklin, Charles, (2007). "Zogby Internet Poll Trial Heats are Odd." *Pollster.com*. (November 27th) www.pollster.com/blogs/zogby_internet_poll_trail_heat.php

Harris Interactive. 2008. Election Results Further Validate Efficacy of Harris Interactive's Online Methodology. (November, 2009) www.harrisinteractive.com/news/allnewsbydate.asp?NewsID=1347

National Council on Public Polls. 2008. NCPP Analysis of Final Presidential Pre-Election Polls, (December, 2008). www.ncpp.org/files/NCPP_2008_analysis_of_election_polls_121808%20pdf_0.pdf

E-Voter Institute On
Elections Are No Longer A One Day Sale

Early voting by absentee or mail-in ballot is becoming increasingly popular. How are those who choose to vote early different from other voters and non-voters and what are the best ways to reach them?

Overall, 131.26 million voters, or 63 percent of the estimated eligible voting-age population, cast ballots for president, up from 60.6 percent in 2004. It is the highest turnout since 1960, when 64.8 percent of eligible voters voted, according to Curtis Gans, Director, Center for the Study of the American Electorate at American University, who tabulated final and official returns from all 50 states and the District of Columbia. It also was the third consecutive presidential election marked by a jump in turnout. It is estimated that between 25-33% of the vote nationwide was cast as a mail-in or absentee ballot.

Results from the E-Voter Institute post election 2008 survey shows that those who voted early through the mail or other means were significantly more inclined to use all web tools, seemed to be slightly more interested in the Internet in general, and had the highest expectations that information about candidates and initiatives would be on the Internet.

For those who voted early, the official web site was almost as attention getting as a television or cable ad. These early voters also favored the Internet as a means for candidates to get their attention. More than one-third of the early voters submitted an email address to a candidate in order to receive a newsletter or updates.

Voter Expectations for Candidate Internet Use (by those who did/did not vote in 2008 election)			
Internet Activities	Voted at the poll	Voted absentee/ mail-in	Did not vote
Official web site	85%	87%	73%
Fund raising	67%	72%	55%
E-mail	66%	70%	55%
Online ads	61%	63%	60%
Webcasts of events	59%	65%	51%
Blogs and podcasts	46%	51%	39%
Television ads on the official web site	64%	62%	58%
Campaign web video on other sites	60%	60%	55%
Participate in social networking sites	33%	35%	26%

E-Voter Institute 2008 Post Election Voter Survey

CHAPTER 13

Do Voter's Have Privacy Rights?

Shaun Dakin

The short answer is: No.

In every election cycle voters across the nation, but particularly in "battleground" states, have their privacy invaded as they are deluged by an increasing number of political communication tools and channels.

Most voters are sick and tired of campaign commercials, but if they don't want to see them they can simply turn off their television or radio. They have that choice.

Not so with automated phone calls or "robo calls". There is no way for the voter to stop their phones from ringing as more and more campaigns turn to robo calls as their primary channel to communicate to voters.

Why? Because while commercial organizations are required by law to respect the privacy rights of consumers, politicians at the federal level and in all but a few states have exempted themselves from these laws. More than 160 million phone numbers have been placed on the National Do Not Call Registry, which requires commercial organizations to stop calling consumers within 30 days of those consumers listing their numbers.

Political campaigns call many of those 160 million numbers with impunity every election cycle. As the spokesperson for millions of voters inundated by political campaigns, I have testified before the Senate Rules Committee in support of the Robocall Privacy Act. Our members report receiving as many as 15 robocalls a day during election season. Mothers have their babies awakened from naps. Night-shift workers who sleep during the day can't get the rest they need. Seniors and others fear that a health emergency could occur while their phone is tied up. Young people have their cell phone minutes used up as well.

Of course, most campaign expenditures go into paid media and most of those resources are poured into television and radio. In fact, according to eMarketer in 2008 50 – 80% of campaign budgets were spent on broadcast television advertising. While only 1-2% of political ad budgets were spent online. Why should commercial companies be required by law to stop invading the privacy of potential customers while politicians are allowed to do whatever they wish to reach potential voters?

The real reason for their personal exemptions is obvious: Politicians write the laws, and politicians like regulation only when it applies to someone else.

The Obama campaign, rightfully, received a great deal of positive press for generating grass roots support and volunteer activity on an unprecedented scale.

The dirty little secret in politics, however, is that the majority of the other 7,000 plus Federal, state and local campaigns in the 08 cycle, up and down the ballot, outsourced their volunteer and grassroots activity to the Internet and automated phone calls or robo calls. Indeed, according to the PEW Center for People and the Press, Robocalls are now the top type of campaign outreach. According to this April 2008 study, 44% of all voters received robo calls.

The study states: For political campaigns, robo-calls are an inexpensive way to reach large numbers of voters. In the March survey, slightly more voters said they had received robo-calls than said they received campaign mailings (39% vs. 36%). In addition, more than twice as many voters said they had gotten a campaign call with a pre-recorded message as said they had gotten a personal campaign call (16%)

If you think that politicians use robo calls because they work, you are wrong.

All third party legitimate data clearly shows that robo calls simply do not work for the primary purpose that they have: to Get Out The Vote (GOTV). In fact, Green and Gerber (Yale) have been studying various forms of political communications for over ten years and have concluded, " … exhibit another robust finding: they are chronically ineffective and inefficient means of mobilizing voters."

So, why do politicians and the consultants that work for them continue to do robo calls?

Unfortunately, the unsatisfying answer is that they continue to do them because they can.

This invasion of privacy has now moved to the Internet with sophisticated databases, mapping tools, and telecommunications technology.

Last September, for example, I received an email from the Obama campaign that had the subject line: "Your Neighbors." Intrigued, I opened the message and learned that the campaign was launching a sophisticated program called "Neighbor-to-Neighbor" that makes "it easier than ever to connect with potential supporters in your community by phone or door-to-door." It continues: "Neighbor-to-Neighbor gives you the option to make phone calls or knock on doors -- the choice is yours."

I thought, "The choice may be mine, but what about my neighbors, who may not want me to bother them at their homes?"

This new technology was both tech-cool and privacy-rights-scary. When I clicked through to myBarackObama.com, I was able to create "walk lists" using a Google map showing me exactly where potential Obama supporters near me live. The Web site provided the names, addresses and phone numbers of these targeted neighbors and offered a prompt for printing out the list. The last step? Log back in and record the results of your "door-to-door" conversations with voters.

I don't know about you, but I do not want my neighbors knocking on my door asking me whom I'm going to vote for. I certainly do not want my name, address and phone number printed on a Google map for the world to see. And, without a doubt, I do not want anyone calling me at home during dinner.

This is an invasion of privacy, because these voters never explicitly gave their permission to have them targeted in a database that invites their neighbors to walk "door to door" to try to persuade them to vote for a particular candidate.

When I tried to opt out of this tool, I learned that while I could opt out of campaign e-mail spam on MyBarackObama.com, there was no way that I could quickly, securely and comprehensively opt out of voter communications that I did not want to receive.

What I could attempt to do was this:
- Log into MBO.com
- Find my local Obama campaign office
- Call my local Obama campaign office and talk to whomever answered the phone (a volunteer) and ask them to remove me from there 1) call list 2) canvassing list and 3) email list
- Hope that somehow this volunteer is able to figure out how to opt me out of campaign communications

There was no way to get a confirmation email that this had, in fact, occurred. Of course, it did not occur. How could it?

John McCain's Web site was very much the same: It provided no mechanism for voters to opt out of unwanted communications other than e-mail.

So what can be done?

It is time for a Voter Privacy Bill of Rights to be introduced and passed by the Congress.

This Voter Privacy Bill of Rights would be built on a single, straightforward principle: Voters should have the right to opt out of all direct political communications that they do not want to receive. Period.

How would this work?

It would start with the existing Federal Do Not Call Registry (DNC). As mentioned earlier, there are over 160 million phone numbers on the Do Not Call list. It would be very easy to change the sign up process in a simple, but effective, way: *Add a button to the DNC website so that voters could opt-out of Political Phone Calls as well as commercial phone calls.* That way, voters could have a choice as to whether they want to receive robo calls from politicians, PACs, Unions, 527's, and local, state, and national parties.

To be very clear, we are not advocating for a ban on political speech. The Constitution and the First Amendment clearly protect politicians right to say what they want. However, the Constitution does not give politicians the right to wake you and your baby up, to disturb your Grandmother living home alone, or to use up your cell phone minutes without your permission.

The Voter Privacy Bill Of Rights would start with amending the Do Not Call Registry to add political calls to the existing regulations. The cost to change the process at donotcall.gov would be minimal and the additional data field to be added to the DNC database would be immaterial to the overall program.

In this hour of economic crisis, when politicians are fighting over terms like capitalism, socialism and nationalization, it would be a simple and effective action to take by Congress to bring a sense of Privacy back to the American voter.

Do it now.

Best Practices

So, you are a campaign manager or candidate that has run out of options and has to go to the "phones" for whatever objective you may have. You may need to get people to an event, to persuade them to vote for a candidate or an issue, or you may simply be reminding them (like they don't know) that there is an election "tomorrow".

What can you do to ensure that you have a better chance to get the word out without it backfiring as voters cringe every time the phone rings?

Use an accurate caller ID: Nothing angers a voter more than receiving a call in which the caller ID name is "spoofed" or inaccurate. It is a deception. And, would you like your campaign brand to be considered as deceptive?

Call only between 9 AM and 8 PM: This should be the law. No telemarketing calls should be made before 9 AM or after 8 PM local time. If you want to ensure your potential voter has hostile feelings towards your campaign, go ahead and call them after hours.

Clearly identify at the beginning of the call who is paying for the call: "This is an automated call from Obama for America"

Give your voter a way to opt-out of future phone calls: "Your privacy is important to Candidate Smith. To ensure that you no longer receive important campaign calls simply press 1. If you would like to received additional calls simply hang up."

Call once a day, at the most: In some recent campaigns, candidates made 3-4 calls a day as the election nears. Guess what? You'll lose any voters you may have had if you call more than once a day. Best practice? Call once a week.

For the most forward thinking, scrub your call list against the Federal Do Not Call Registry or the National Political Do Not Contact Registry (NPDNC). Voters don't distinguish between telemarketers calling for auto warranties and candidates calling for votes. Voters can try to stop auto warranty calls; they would like candidates to honor their request not to be called.

Predictions

Voters will turn the tables on candidates. After years of taking it, voters will start to utilize technology that allows them to robo call representatives on issues that they care about. Imagine if a voter could sign up for a service that robo-called representatives about the issues that they care about using their specific name and address.

An automated call could go like this: "Hi Representative Smith this is Shaun Dakin a constituent that lives at 1235 LakeWood Drive, Middletown, OH 12345. I'm calling you to ask that you support HR 123 and vote yes for Veteran Benefits. Paid for by the Veteran Association of America."

Voters will demand to be compensated for their time. Imagine: You would have access to a list of voters who wanted to be called and agreed to listen to the entire automated message; if you paid them for their time. If you want to call a voter on their cell phone or home phone you will be able to call those voters that have Opted In to receiving calls as long as they are paid for their time. There will be an "opt in" list of voters that have agreed to receive robo calls from candidates and listen to the message as long as they are compensated for their time.

Political calls will be added to the Do Not Call Registry(s): Sooner or later politicians will do the right thing and add political robo calls to the do not call registry. Sick of alienating voters and getting robo called themselves, politicians will decide that enough is enough and do the unthinkable: regulate themselves.

REFERENCES

www.marketingcharts.com/television/just-2-of-political-ad-budgets-to-be-spent-online-4757/

http://pewresearch.org/pubs/785/robo-calls-election-2008

http://pewresearch.org/pubs/785/robo-calls-election-2008

http://research.yale.edu/GOTV/?q=node/10

CHAPTER 14

Creating the
Modern Campaign

Ben Katz

Ten years ago, there was a legitimate question of whether the Internet had a role to play in political campaigns. That question has been decided.

The Internet is here. Nearly 80% of Americans use email. Over half of U.S. homes have broadband connections and wireless access is common and growing.

As for political campaigns, the Internet has been accepted. Asking if a campaign uses email is now nearly as absurd as asking if they use the telephone. The question is not if they're using the Internet, but what elements are they using, how much do they use it, and what's working for them?

During the 2008 cycle, my company, CompleteCampaigns.com provided online campaign management tools to over 1000 campaigns ranging from Presidential to local school boards. In doing this, we were able to see first hand how they were using the Internet.

Campaign use of the Internet broke down into three main areas: internal uses, engaging supporters and persuasion efforts. In this paper, I'll provide a brief overview of what we have observed in each of these areas and compare that to the recent results from the E-Voter Institute's 2008 Survey of Voter Expectations.

Internal Uses

Within campaign teams, there has been massive adoption of Internet tools and applications for communication. The Internet is now the core of any modern campaign's infrastructure.

Email

Most significantly, we have seen the acceptance of email as a primary communication tool within the campaign team. Email has become the primary method for transfer of information and reports within the campaign team. Consultants send polling results, mail piece proofs, draft fundraising letters and nearly everything else imaginable via email.

Staff and volunteers can be managed in large part remotely using information transfer over e-mail. Last minute updates can be sent out with very little lead time or cost.

News sites and blogs

We are also seeing our clients increasingly turn to online news sources, including both blogs and the websites of traditional news outlets as a primary source of information.

While newspapers and TV are still monitored, the online outlets are often the first source of breaking news about a campaign. Aggregation tools, like Google Alerts (www.google.com/alerts) and Technorati (technorati.com) allow campaigns to receive instant notification about key news that can impact their race.

Web-Based Solutions

The Internet is no longer just a faster way to exchange information from one party to another. There are now web-based applications to replace desktop software for almost any purpose, and campaign management is no exception. In 2000, few, if any, campaigns were using any web-based tools. Now, the majority of Congressional campaigns are using at least one online application, as are many who are running for state or local office. There are hundreds of tools available for a wide variety of campaign needs.

Engaging Supporters
Email & Fundraising

As with internal communication, for engaging supporters, email has become the most important and most widely used method of communication. It's cheap, widely used and rapid.

It's also shown itself to be amazing effective for on-line fundraising. The record breaking online fundraising numbers shown by the Presidential campaigns, and mirrored on the smaller scale, by state and local campaigns have primarily been driven by email. Most critically, this is widely accepted by campaign supporters. Of the "very political active" respondents of the E-Voter Institute 2008 research, over 75% of those 18+ expected candidates to use the Internet for both fundraising and email.

Finding Supporters

Although the 2008 cycle is still underway, it appears that the major online success falls in the intersection between engaging supporters and persuading. Rather, as the Obama and McCain campaigns have already realized, nearly every candidate has a large number of unknown supporters. Both of these Presidential committees have embarked on revenue positive online advertising campaigns seeking to identify and engage these "invisible supporters." While local candidates lack the name recognition that Presidential candidate hold, the E-Voter/HCD survey suggests that this model should work on the local level as well.

Distributed Campaigning

There has been an explosive growth of distributed campaigning tools since 2004. The use of online systems allows campaign supporters to contact voters and otherwise assist the campaign without coming into the campaign office. Both major parties have pushed online systems that have allowed party activist easy access to voter lists for persuasion and GOTV efforts.

Persuasion

Voter persuasion remains the holy grail of online politics: repeatedly rumored and sought but as of yet, unfound and unproven. The E-Voter Institute 2008 survey shows that the less politically active someone is, the less likely they are to want to be contacted by candidates via online methods. For example, while 37% of the very politically active thought that email was a good way for the candidate to contact them, only 15% of the "not engaged other than voting" thought that was a good way to contact them. Conversely, 64% of the not engaged thought TV or cable ads were a good way to contact versus 61% of the very active.

2008 Political Ads Worth $2.5 Billion to $2.7 Billion

TNS Media Intelligence: TV takes $2.2 billion, more expected in 2009.

By Claire Atkinson

Broadcasting & Cable, December 2, 2008

Save for a few ongoing races, tallies for political ad spending in 2008 have been finalized: Between $2.5 billion and $2.7 billion were spent on political ads this election season, according to figures from ad measurement company TNS Media Intelligence. Television took the lion's share, with $2.2 billion. The total figure is slightly short of the projected $3 billion take, in part because of a shortened general election season, but up from $1.7 billion back in 2004. In what will no doubt be welcome news for beleaguered TV executives, political ad dollars are

expected to continue to flow in 2009.

"2009 is going to be another record setting cycle," said Evan Tracey, president of the political ad tracking unit, Campaign Media Analysis Group, part of ad measurement company TNS Media Intelligence. "There's no reason to think there's going to be any decline."

As President-elect Barack Obama continues to fill out his cabinet with existing senators and governors, there'll be a lot of jockeying at the local level to replace them. Tracey reports that there are some 36 governor races in 2010. Issue advocacy is also predicted to be big business in

2009 as groups do table setting for issue fights on healthcare down the line.

For 2008, however, TNS figures suggest broadcast as usual took the vast majority of TV's $2.2 billion take. "Broadcast TV should come in around $2 billion," Tracey said, "While national cable and national networks was around $200 million." Print, radio, online and local cable is expected to share the remaining $200 million to $400 million, he said.

The long Democratic primary run-off truncated the general election which ran for four months, rather than the eight months in the 2004 presidential election, to which Tracey attributed the slight short in spending in 2008. While the campaigns had plenty of money to spend, the final totals are disappointing in that they fell short of the expected $3 billion that TNS had projected earlier this year. Still radio and local cable benefited from a surfeit of dollars.

"Candidates had more money than there was broadcast time to buy," Tracey said.

www.broadcastingcable.com/article/print/160115-2008_Political_Ads_Worth_2_5_ ...
4/21/2009

CHAPTER 15

Why Political Consultants Are So Nervous

Karen A.B. Jagoda

Pity the poor political consultants, fundraisers, media strategists, pollsters and professional organizers. The ground is shifting under their feet and they are struggling in vain to maintain their balance.

Those who have latched onto the Internet in a half-hearted way now claim they are the experts in multi-media campaigns. Those who insist that they have the secret sauce for success in online fundraising or raising awareness hold their cards close to their vest. They reap high fees for their deep insights that are nothing more than experiments, as there is little history of what works and the environment keeps changing. Lucky perhaps or just in the right place at the right time, these political consultants still fiercely protect the way things have always been done. Even the ones who consistently lose races boast of their prowess.

Money is the draw and these consultants are not likely to give up their fees, media commissions and retainers just because the Internet is changing the way voters perceive candidates and causes. It will take the consistent winning by unknown but web-savvy candidates to break this cabal of those who deem themselves the deciders of who is an acceptable candidate.

How Do Voters Decide

E-Voter Institute 2008 research confirmed that television still has the most impact on how all voters make up their minds about who to vote for, though the Internet is not far behind. This holds true across party and gender lines.

One out of three voters say television has the most effect on their voting decision while one in five say the Internet is their information source. When looking at all of the survey respondents were most Internet proficient, those less politically active individuals report they are most likely to be swayed to vote for candidates based on television advertising and the Internet. There is a similar trend among those more politically active, though this group is twice as likely to rely on recommendations from the party.

Most Effect on Voting Decision By Political Affiliation and by Gender						
		Political affiliation			Gender	
Influences	Total	Dem	Rep	Ind	M	F
Who my family votes for	7%	6%	10%	5%	6%	7%
Internet information	21%	20%	19%	24%	27%	18%
Television	34%	38%	30%	32%	29%	37%
Newspaper editorials	6%	6%	5%	7%	6%	6%
Recommendations from my political party	5%	6%	9%	2%	6%	5%
Friends	5%	5%	4%	5%	5%	5%
Direct mail	2%	2%	2%	2%	2%	2%
Phone calls from campaign volunteers	0%	1%	0%	0%	0%	0%
Endorsements	3%	3%	3%	3%	3%	3%

E-Voter Institute 2008 Third Annual Survey of Voter Expectations

Voters whose ideological beliefs are moderate, somewhat liberal or somewhat conservative are significantly more likely to report that they are swayed by television advertising than voters who identify themselves as very liberal or very conservative.

Most Effect on Voting Decision By Political ideology			
Influences	Very Liberal	Moderate	Very Conservative
Who my family votes for	6%	6%	15%
Internet information	26%	20%	16%
Television	31%	36%	24%
Newspaper editorials	5%	7%	4%
Recommendations from my political party	8%	4%	10%
Friends	6%	5%	5%
Direct mail	2%	2%	3%
Phone calls from campaign volunteers	1%	0%	1%
Endorsements	2%	3%	2%

E-Voter Institute 2008 Third Annual Survey of Voter Expectations

The post election 2008 E-Voter Institute survey of voters shows similarities and interesting differences between ethnic groups when it comes to persuasive sources of information.

Debates seem to appeal to all groups though this might be a result of people saying the "right" answer as opposed to what really influenced their decisions. We have seen similar results in studies where people are asked what television channels they watch and a disproportionate number claim they tune into PBS.

Influence	Caucasian	Hispanic	African-American	Asian
Most Effect on Voting Decision				
By Ethnic Group				
Who my family voted for	8%	8%	9%	16%
Internet information	37%	39%	34%	50%
Television/cable advertisements	19%	36%	31%	28%
Television/cable news reports and commentators	36%	44%	39%	45%
Debates	55%	65%	66%	53%
Newspaper editorials	15%	20%	15%	23%
Recommendations from my political party	11%	14%	14%	11%
Friends	14%	23%	15%	23%
Direct mail	5%	14%	9%	12%
Phone calls from campaign volunteers	2%	5%	9%	8%
Endorsements	9%	16%	17%	17%

E-Voter Institute 2008 Post Election Survey of Voter Expectations

Achieving Political Goals

According to the E-Voter 2008 surveys, nine out of ten consultants think that the Internet successfully addresses fundraising and volunteer recruitment from the loyal base, while three out of five consultants see the Internet effective for increasing name recognition with swing, Independent and undecided voters.

Consultants believe that the most effective uses of the Internet for reaching the loyal base are fundraising, recruiting volunteers, announcing events, and rapid response. Name recognition and persuasion are seen as the most advantageous uses of the Internet to reach swing, Independent and undecided voters.

Goal	Loyal Base	Swing and Crossover	Ind	Undcd
Fundraising	94%	35%	28%	15%
GOTV	77%	47%	37%	28%
Identify Potential Voters	35%	61%	58%	51%
Build Contact Lists	78%	57%	47%	34%
Persuasion	27%	67%	59%	56%
Name Recognition	40%	70%	63%	67%
Impact Favorability	47%	57%	50%	51%
Rapid Response	83%	38%	30%	30%
Build Relationships	66%	54%	44%	34%
Recruit Volunteers	92%	29%	20%	10%
Announce Events	88%	52%	42%	40%
Build Momentum	69%	45%	39%	31%

Constituents Best Addressed by Internet Consultants View by Target Voters

E-Voter Institute 2008 Seventh Annual Survey of Political and Advocacy Communications Leaders

There are distinct differences in the way that those who work with Democrats and those who work with Republicans see the use of the Internet for targeting the loyal base and the more unpredictable voters. The Democrats are 50% more likely than the Republicans to use the Internet to identify potential voters in the loyal base and use the Internet for rapid response to reach undecided voters. On the other hand, Republicans are 28% more likely to use the Internet to build relationships with Independent voters.

Consultant Hesitations

According to E-Voter Institute 2008 research, the vast majority of the consultants think the Internet is effective for reaching the loyal base now and certainly by 2012. Most are optimistic on the effectiveness of reaching swing, Independent and undecided voters with Internet technologies between now and 2012.

E-Voter Institute research indicates significant growth from 2006 to 2008 in the acceptance by consultants of the Internet for reaching the loyal base as well as the swing, Independent and undecided voters.

But still one third of the consultants have hesitations about using the Internet with interesting differences by party.

Consultants and Hesitations to Use Web				
	Total Consultants	Dem	Rep	Ind
Hesitations	65%	64%	75%	76%
No Hesitations	35%	36%	25%	24%

E-Voter Institute 2008 Seventh Annual Survey of Political and Advocacy Communications Leaders

Political Consultants View of the Internet

With a sprinkle of social media hipness, a candidate or advocate can Twitter, blog, or post video on YouTube but the magic just does not happen. While political consultants themselves use web tools, they are still convinced that those methods are not the best way to reach swing voters, minorities and independents.

The gap between what consultants are recommending versus what voters are expecting is hard to explain as the consultants themselves are using the Internet extensively though not playing as many online games.

E-Voter Institute survey results from 2008 compare what consultants think works best with the loyal base and swing voters to what voters expect candidates to do on the Internet. The results reveal significant lag in acceptance by consultants of all web tools.

Looking at what consultants think works and what voters claim are the best way to get their attention shows that again consultants are missing some of the signs from voters about how to break through the media clutter in their lives.

Most noteworthy in the E-Voter Institute 2008 survey results are the underuse of yard signs, debates, and newspaper ads, and over reliance on phone and direct mail. On the Internet, political consultants under-estimate the value of candidate web sites, online ads, and webcasts, and perhaps over-estimate the value of email.

It is also very revealing to see what consultants think works versus what people have done online related to politics. There is more evidence that consultants over-estimate the likelihood of getting opt-in emails and online contributions and under-estimate the interest voters have in finding information on their own. *Note that in the following chart the consultants were limited to the top 3 most effective ways to reach voters while voters were able to select all that applied.*

Consultants and Voters By Activities

Activities	Effective for reaching loyal base Top 3	Effective for reaching swing and Independent Top 3	Voter say best ways to get their attention (All that apply)
TV/Cable ads	26%	52%	63%
Debates	9%	31%	57%
Candidate web site	25%	22%	51%
Word of mouth	28%	29%	39%
Direct mail	38%	37%	31%
Newspaper ads	4%	5%	29%
Radio ads	8%	16%	26%
Online ads	5%	11%	25%
Email	46%	13%	22%
Webcasts	4%	3%	20%
Yard signs/outdoor billboards	3%	4%	20%
Blogs and podcasts	8%	4%	16%
Social networking sites	10%	11%	15%
Online video	7%	11%	14%
Phone	29%	16%	9%

E-Voter Institute 2008 Seventh Annual Survey of Political and Advocacy Communications Leaders

Looking deeper at the skills of the political consultants we see a correlation between their use of the Internet and their interest in using the Internet for clients. Is this a question of just not enough education or a lack of interest in learning new skills? If the consultants don't use the tools, how can they recommend them?

Internet Behavior of Consultants By Consultant Client Types				
Online Activities	Total Consultants	Dem	Rep	Ind
Use email	98%	98%	98%	100%
Read newspapers or magazines online	92%	91%	90%	87%
Have broadband access to the Internet at home	88%	90%	90%	95%
Forward links and email to friends/ family	87%	86%	87%	97%
Make online purchases	87%	87%	87%	84%
Have wireless capability	76%	79%	71%	74%
Download video and/or audio	71%	74%	65%	71%
Social network member	69%	69%	62%	61%
Post ratings or comments online	57%	57%	48%	39%
Listen to online radio	46%	47%	40%	39%
Post to other blogs	45%	41%	41%	42%
Subscribe to RSS feeds	45%	44%	41%	47%
Maintain a blog or your own web site	44%	46%	41%	50%
Upload video and/or audio	42%	36%	38%	45%
Use widgets	30%	27%	33%	32%
Play online games	21%	22%	16%	18%
Use Twitter or other micro-blogging sites	20%	19%	22%	16%

E-Voter Institute 2008 Seventh Annual Survey of Political and Advocacy Communications Leaders

Reaching Voters Across the Political Spectrum

E-Voter Institute research in 2007 and 2008 indicates that consultants
consider the Internet a more effective tool for reaching liberal activists
than for reaching social conservatives. This may change as social
conservatives become more sophisticated in their use of online tools and
come to expect that their candidates reach them through those means.

Methods Effective Reaching Liberals

Methods	2007 All Consultants	2008 All Consultants
E-mail	76%	88%
Candidate web site	74%	79%
Social networking sites	65%	77%
Blogs and podcasts	77%	75%
Events with candidate or surrogate	75%	74%
Online video	72%	73%
Online ads	64%	69%
Word of mouth	66%	67%
Debates	70%	66%
Webcasts	63%	65%
Text messaging	53%	58%
Direct mail	61%	54%
TV/Cable ads	62%	52%
Phone	51%	49%
Radio ads	40%	46%
Newspaper ads	42%	43%
Yard signs/billboards	38%	36%

*E-Voter Institute 2008 Seventh Annual Survey of Political and
Advocacy Communications Leaders*

Methods Effective Reaching Social Conservatives

Methods	2007 All Consultants	2008 All Consultants
Radio ads	71%	70%
Events with candidate or surrogate	76%	69%
E-mail	63%	67%
Candidate web site	65%	66%
Direct mail	74%	62%
Debates	75%	62%
TV/Cable ads	70%	61%
Word of mouth	66%	61%
Phone	59%	56%
Newspaper ads	62%	48%
Blogs and podcasts	47%	47%
Online ads	51%	45%
Yard signs/outdoor billboards	50%	43%
Online video	46%	43%
Social networking sites	33%	43%
Webcasts	40%	34%
Text messaging	21%	19%

E-Voter Institute 2008 Seventh Annual Survey of Political and Advocacy Communications Leaders

Reaching Social Network Members

Consultants don't seem to appreciate how much members of social networks expect candidates to use the Internet for a variety of activities and therefore seem to underestimate the impact on both loyal and swing voters.

- Seven out of ten active social net members expect to see online ads for candidates while only 5% of consultants think online ads are effective for reaching the loyal base and 11% think they are effective to reach swing, Independent and undecided voters.
- Two out of three of all social net members expect webcasts of events while only 4% of consultants think webcasts are useful for reaching the loyal base and even less (3%) think that webcasts are effective for reaching swing voters.
- Seven out of ten active social net members expect campaign web video on sites other than the official candidate site while only 7% of consultants think this is an effective way to reach the base and 11% think this is a way to find swing, Independent and undecided voters.

Voter Expectations and View From Consultants

Activities	Voters			Consultants	
	Total Voters	Member Updates Often	Non-Member	Effective to Reach Loyal Base	Effective to Reach Other Voters
Official web site	87%	90%	83%	25%	22%
Online ads	65%	72%	61%	5%	11%
Webcasts of events	62%	67%	58%	4%	3%
E-mail	60%	68%	57%	46%	13%
Campaign video on other sites	60%	70%	54%	7%	11%
Blogs and podcasts	55%	64%	49%	8%	4%
Participate in social networking sites	38%	59%	29%	10%	11%

E-Voter Institute 2008 Third Annual Survey of Voter Expectations and Seventh Annual Survey of Political and Advocacy Communications Leaders

As new online tools become available, social network members will be an even greater force for both the campaign as well as the opposition in both official and non-official ways.

CHAPTER 16

Online Video:
Window on the World

Tony Winders

The use of online video in the political process has grown steadily in recent years, to the point of being ubiquitous in the 2008 election and with no signs slowing down in the years to come.

The explosion of video has been driven mainly by faster consumer Internet connection speeds, the pervasiveness of video capture devices and the availability of relatively inexpensive web video production, editing, hosting and streaming. Combined with a wider segment of the population being comfortable with video as viable a means of communication, a perfect storm has been created for the use of video as a meaningful part of the political process online.

The first use of video in online presidential campaigns appeared in 2004, but was relegated primarily to repurposed television spots appearing on candidates' web sites. The primary catalyst for their awareness was e-mail to send links to the videos, which would in turn create a viral effect of people passing them along to friends, resulting in earned media exposure if and when the spots were talked about in mainstream media.

One such example was the Bush-Cheney reelection campaign's effort to define Kerry as pawn of special interests before the general election. It was the first time during a presidential race that a Web-only video attack ad was sent via e-mail, which was said to have been distributed to six million supporters.

At the onset of the 2008 election cycle, which began earlier than any before it, it was unclear how much of a role video would play in electing the 44th president of the United States. After all, it was little more than a footnote in the 2004 election, during which the Web was defined more by Howard Dean's fundraising and grassroots mobilization efforts.

As it turned out, video significantly impacted the candidates' ability to communicate directly with the electorate, the public's ability to engage with candidates in creative new ways and as a tactic for stakeholders of all kinds to express themselves in the interest of their candidates of choice. A wide variety of video content, with an equally broad range of production values, was proffered up by the candidates themselves. In addition, several independent groups and individuals promoted their candidates through unauthorized campaigns of their own.

The result was a highly energized campaign that would become the turning point for the use of Internet video in political campaigns and the basis from which future elections will be measured. While relatively little investment was made in video advertising online, and the impact of video overall was difficult to attribute directly to the success or failure of any single candidate, it was still an undeniable force in the electoral process that was as entertaining as it was effective.

Classifying Video

The term "video" is so all-encompassing that it is helpful to classify and further define the ways in which video has been used effectively in online political campaigns. In the nonlinear, multimedia world in which we now live, video includes animation and television content that makes its way online, video that only appears on a candidate's site and television-style spots that intentionally cross the line with the intent of being spread virally and talked about in the 24-hour cable news cycle.

The YouTube phenomenon, which provides an instant distribution mechanism and empowers everyone to be a journalist, has added to the empowerment of individuals and groups to have a voice in the political process through use of video. Adding to the proliferation of video as a significant communication force is its ability to be distributed easily across social networks, via e-mail and on mobile devices in addition to personal computers.

As flexible as the medium itself, are the ways in which political campaigns have used video as a means for communicating with constituents, shaping public opinion and attacking opponents. Not to mention the unintended consequences of citizen journalism and the unauthorized campaigns of special interest groups, celebrities and individuals.

While the examples here focus predominantly on candidates' use of video, examples also exist for how political action committees and independent groups supporting ballot initiatives have successfully used the medium to communicate their objectives, and most of the tactics described in this chapter can be used to that end.

Candidates Use of Video

To understand how online video is being used effectively in political campaigns, a helpful starting point is a review of the wide range of ways candidates have employed it in recent elections. From the most basic tactic of candidates speaking directly to voters from their own sites, to repurposing spots that appeared on television, to mobilizing constituents and developing ads exclusively for online advertising, candidates are experimenting with various ways to use video to achieve a wide range of political marketing objectives.

Here are examples of how candidates have successfully used video online in recent years.

For communicating with voters: In January, 2007, Hillary Clinton officially announced her candidacy for president on her site, hillaryclinton.com. In the video, she stated that she was not just starting a campaign, but beginning a dialogue with the American people and invited them to a series of online video chats in the weeks that followed. www.youtube.com/watch?v=5M66J3th2Ns

For mobilizing the base: Barack Obama used video to communicate with his constituents by regularly posting video updates on the web, but his campaign went a step further. A video posted by Amy Hamblin gave passionate members of Obama's base a tour of MyBO.com and how to use the social media and networking tools available to them on the site. This simple instructional video played a significant, though understated role in Obama's effective use of the web for community building that would ultimately help him win the 2008 presidential election. www.youtube.com/watch?v=uRY720HE0DE

For attacking opponents: Some broadcast-quality political ads are made with no intention of ever appearing on television, either because they are too controversial, because the group producing them does not have the budget to buy television time, or both. In one case, an ad wasn't shown online either, but the mere awareness of its existence within even a small group created a stir that generated attention throughout national news media and the blogosphere.

One such spot not seen on TV, but used online to stir controversy and earned media coverage was a Bush attack on Kerry in 2004. www.nytimes.com/2004/02/22/weekinreview/22rute.html

Although it did appear on television, perhaps the most famous of all attack ads which was circulated extensively online, was "Any

Questions?," a spot produced by Swift Boat Veterans for Truth during the 2004 campaign which called into question John Kerry's war hero status and fueled constant news coverage of the topic throughout August, 2004.

www.youtube.com/watch?v=V4Zk9YmED48

True Majority Action PAC produced a spoof of The Apprentice reality television program called "Trump Fires Bush," in which embarrassing footage of George W. Bush is edited with scenes from the show. While the ad may have been too juvenile to makes its way onto television, the spot was seen by millions online.

www.youtube.com/watch?v=5fKPKhXFxs4

MoveOn.org developed a series of ads called "Real People." Produced in the same testimonial style of Apple's "Switch" ads, by its creator Errol Morris, the spots featured real people who voted for George W. Bush in 2000 but were planning to vote for Kerry in 2004 and showcasing serious themes such as a Marine talking about how the war in Iraq wasn't worth his friends' lives.

www.errolmorris.com/html/election04/election04_main.html

For Advertising: While the use of online advertising increased from 2004 to 2008, the amount spent in targeting voters online paled in comparison to television and direct mail. Estimates of total online ad spending during the 2008 campaign ranged from $20 million to $110 million; however video advertising revenue was not of a significant enough amount to be called out separately.

Video advertising online can be delivered via in-stream or in-banner ads. In-stream ads, also known as pre-roll or post-roll ads, are shown immediately preceding or following a video which an online user has requested to play by clicking on the video. In-banner video uses the Flash file format to deliver a video ad within the space of a standard banner ad, typically a 300x250 medium rectangle, as the page loads.

Although audio can be automatically played, the accepted best practice is for audio to be user-initiated.

Ironically, while the ability to measure online advertising effectiveness by way of impressions, clicks and conversions (people donating or signing up) is possible, a lack of empirical evidence of the ability to persuade voters to act differently is one of the reasons it has not become a more mainstream political activity. Other reasons include lack of education, expertise and clear compensation models for political consultants.

The Unauthorized Campaign - Constituent and Celebrity Use of Video

One of the most entertaining uses of video in politics online has been the unauthorized campaign, in which videos are produced by individuals, celebrities or groups operating outside the direct control of the campaigns they support. While thousands of videos are produced in this vain, only a few reach a "viral" status of being passed along to millions and ultimately capturing the attention of consumer media as a result of their popularity.

Consumer examples of unauthorized campaigns

Vote Different – A spoof of the famous 1984 Apple commercial featured Hillary Clinton as big brother and directed viewers to BarackObama.com.
www.youtube.com/watch?v=6h3G-1MZxjo

"I Got a Crush...On Obama" – Created by Barely Political's Ben Relles and featuring "Obama Girl" Amber Lee Ettinger, "I Got a Crush...On Obama" was viewed millions of times online and named the biggest web video of 2007 by People magazine and featured extensively in mainstream media including the Associated Press, Newsweek and major network and cable television news media.
www.youtube.com/watch?v=wKsoXHYICqU

In 2003, the MoveOn.org created the "Bush in 30 Seconds," project, inviting its supporters to create their own political ads. The site attracted more than 1,000 entries, from which the MoveOn.org community selected 15 finalists and the winners were voted on by a celebrity panel of judges. www.bushin30seconds.org

Barack Roll – Hugh Atkin created a popular parody video of the Rickrolling meme entitled "Barack Roll" and featuring of clips from Obama speeches voicing over the entire lyrics to Rick Astley's 1987 hit song "Never Gonna Give You Up." www.metacafe.com/watch/1712091/barack_roll/

Celebrity examples of unauthorized campaigns

Yes We Can – Recording artist will.i.am combined powerful clips from Barak Obama speeches with a resounding lyric "yes we can," which was voiced over by will.i.am and dozens of other celebrities and artists, including John Legend, Kareem Abdul Jabar, Herbie Hancock and Scarlet Johansson. www.youtube.com/watch?v=jjXyqcx-mYY

Paris Hilton used humor to create the launch of a fake campaign ad posted exclusively on Funny Or Die in response to a McCain ad that referenced her celebrity status. In the spot she refers to McCain as "white haired dude" and after communicating her energy policy tells viewers she is thinking of painting the White House pink. www.funnyordie.com/videos/64ad536a6d/paris-hilton-responds-to-mccain-ad-from-paris-hilton-adam-ghost-panther-mckay-and-chris-henchy

Michael J Fox endorsed Clair McCaskill in her bid for United States Senate, calling on Missouri voters to vote for McCaskill and calling out her opponent Jim Talent's opposition to cell research to help fight life threatening diseases. www.youtube.com/watch?v=a9WB_PXjTBo

The Unscripted Campaign - YouTube and the Rise of Citizen Journalism

We live in an age when the technology to record and distribute video images is pervasive, giving anyone the tools to report on everything from politics to plane crashes. In politics, ironically, these unplanned and unbudgeted videos, with their low production value, are potentially the most enlightening and bring a level playing field to democracy that our forefathers could not have predicted and may be just the equalizing force needed to restore the public's trust in the political process today.

Sen. George Allen (R) Macaca Moment – In August, 2006, during a campaign rally, Allen refers to S.R. Sidarth as "Macaca." Sidarth, a man of Indian descent, was videotaping the rally as a volunteer of Democrat challenger James Webb. When the clip was posted on YouTube, it prompted an apology and the negative publicity that ensued contributed to Allen ultimately losing his senate seat. www.youtube.com/watch?v=r90z0PMnKwI

In January, 2008, a video of John McCain's comments during at a Derry, New Hampshire town hall meeting in which he stated his willingness for America to have a presence in Iraq for the next 100 years became a video snafu that was shared extensively online and referenced in political media coverage throughout 2008. www.youtube.com/watch?v=VFknKVjuyNk

Some citizen journalism is not so organic. Here are a few of examples of programmed citizen journalism that took place during the 2008 campaign:

As part of its 2008 election coverage, MTV employed a "street team" of 51 amateur journalists to file blog reports, photos and videos which were syndicated to MTV's mobile web site and the Associated Press Online Video Network. think.mtv.com/Groups/street-team-08/

Video the Vote is a national network of citizen journalists, independent filmmakers, videographers and media professionals working together to document voter suppression and disenfranchisement, with information made publicly available at videothevote.org.

videothevote.org/

PBS teamed up with YouTube to create Video Your Vote, the largest library of Election Day content supplied by voters who recorded the process of casting their own ballots around the U.S.

www.youtube.com/videoyourvote

Corporate/Media Giants

Use of video in the political process is not limited to candidates and citizen journalists. Major media companies have a critical role to play in the use of political video online, as they have the credibility and the audience to quickly mobilize millions of people into action. Although their approach and their motivation may be different from campaigns and individuals, media companies have produced some of the most interesting uses of video in the electoral process.

On television: The CNN-YouTube Presidential Debates – During series of televised debates, presidential hopefuls fielded questions submitted by voters through the video sharing site YouTube. The Democratic Party debate took place in Charleston, South Carolina on July 23, 2007. The Republican Party debate took place in St. Petersburg, Florida on November 28, 2007.

In addition to the unique use of the web to collect questions that would filtered by an editorial team and aired on live television, the events also generated news for their answers. During the Democratic debate, Obama's reply to one question stated his willingness to meet with leaders of Iran, Syria and North Korea, creating a stir that would carry through the election. During the Republican debate, a controversy arose from a question asked of Hillary Clinton by retired general Keith Kerr, an adviser to her campaign who, whether planted by the Clinton campaign or chosen by CNN editors, was a misstep which made news in and of itself.

www.youtube.com/user/YTdebates

On the Internet: The popular video sharing site YouTube, created "YouChoose '08," a voter education initiative that allowed candidates to inform millions of potential voters through video. Candidates were invited to develop their own channels and political videos of all types, including campaign videos, speeches, informal chats, behind-the-scenes footage and more were featured throughout the election cycle. In turn, viewers were invited to provide video responses, text comments and ratings.

www.youtube.com/youchoose

Practical Application

So what can one do with this understanding of the video landscape, and what is required at a practical level to repeat the successes and avoid the failures of prior campaigns? How much does it cost and where does one begin to formulate an Internet video strategy?

Ironically, the most powerful and influential use of video typically costs nothing and is produced far outside of the control of the campaign. After all, video captured on a mobile phone and uploaded to YouTube, or an unintentional slip of the tongue, can have as profound an effect on the outcome of a campaign as a polished television commercial backed by millions in media spending.

Unfortunately, the ability to create a viral effect for a video is difficult to contrive, and is led mainly by its entertainment value or controversial nature. Still, video can and should be an integral part of any campaign's Internet strategy, whether from the standpoint of giving the candidate an interactive platform from which to communicate directly with constituents or as part of an intentional grassroots marketing program.

Conclusion

If the 2008 presidential election cycle is any indication, the use of video in the electoral process is here to stay and will become increasingly more sophisticated as the medium evolves and more political consultants learn to use it for achieving a wide range of political objectives.

Video has always been the most persuasive of all media, and while online advertising may not have registered in a meaningful way in 2008, as it becomes more integral to political marketing, video will play an even more significant role in the years ahead. Irrespective of advertising, the ability for video to inexpensively say so much will mandate it be incorporated at all levels of campaigning and activism, if only on the sites to which all other efforts are directed.

Moreover, everyone from the most engaged members of the electorate, to the sophisticated digital media organizations of major media companies will embrace video for its ability to create interesting dialogue about candidates and issues at all levels of media usage and the social, political and economic spectrum.

While video tools and technology are more pervasive than ever and may have contributed to a more engaged electorate, at what level we push video to its full potential in politics online ultimately rests with individual viewers and would-be citizen journalists. No matter what, video is here to stay and will be one of the most powerful means of online political communication for decades to come.

E-Voter Institute Highlight

Guidelines for the CNN*YouTube Debates held in 2007

- Be original—choose your own approach.
- Be personal—you perspective is important
- Choose your focus—you can address one or all of the candidates
- Keep it quick—your question should be less than 30 seconds (and, in the language of your choice).
- Make it look good—speak loudly and keep that camera steady.
- Provide context—in your question or video description, include your name & home town.
- Please note—all videos are subject to the YouTube Terms of Use.

Viewers were asked to submit video questions for the Democratic and Republican candidates. The CNN political team chose the questions deemed most creative and compelling and they were shown during the debate for the candidates to respond to.

CHAPTER 17

Political Mobile Applications: Uncharted Territory, Fertile Ground

Kathie Legg

The topic for this chapter is the use of mobile phone applications in politics. Here's the problem: it's barely been done. But mobile applications are growing fast, especially in the commercial sector (which will be the main focus here primarily because of the dearth of examples from other sectors). I will also discuss below one of the best examples of a political mobile application: the Obama '08 iPhone application. I think there are opportunities for using mobile applications in the political realm that have yet to be tapped. As you read this chapter, which is designed to give you the foundation needed to create the next big political mobile phone application, keep your creative thinking cap on.

Mobile Phone Applications

A mobile phone is more than just a way to make and receive phone calls on the go. They can be used for a myriad of different purposes, and can be personalized and customized in ways that are unique to individual users.

Recent years have seen a proliferation of mobile applications that aid in this personalization and customization. These mobile applications are added on after the phone is purchased and tap into the phone's core features like GPS location, sound, touch screen, navigational buttons, and video display. They are easy to download and install and vastly expand a phone's capabilities. According to Nielsen Mobile, 13% of mobile phone users over the age of 13 access data through applications, a number that would have been unthinkable a few years ago and one that will likely seem shockingly low a few years from now.

Background on Application Stores

Mobile phone applications are increasingly sold through centralized marketplaces that offer one-stop shopping, which makes dissemination of an application very easy. Apple first introduced its application store in July 2008. Since then, its App Store has been flooded with over 30,000 applications, some offered for free and others charging fees of as much as $20 or more. The store has had over 1 billion downloads in total.

Within the next year Google opened its Android Marketplace. These two entrants in this marketplace opened the floodgates, both in terms of the number of applications created and the revenues generated by them. According to The Neilsen Company, in 2008, total mobile application revenues were about $1 billion.

In-Stat research estimates that more than 100 million application-compatible mobile phones will be shipping within five years.[1]

In the brief period since the introduction of Apple's App Store, it is already tough to find a mobile company that doesn't have its own version of an application store. For example, Nokia has the Ovi Apps Store, Microsoft has the Windows Mobile Skymarket, RIM has the Blackberry Apps Storefront, Palm has the webOS Software Store, AT&T has the Apps Beta, and Samsung has the Mobile Applications store.

The proliferation of applications, application stores, and large revenue numbers from application sales indicates that the mobile applications business is here to stay. The success of mobile applications need not be limited to the for-profit sector. Even non-traditional businesses are getting in on the action - universities like Stanford are even offering courses on mobile phone applications! The political world should not be far behind.

Successful Application Development Tips

Games: Mobile phones have become the main source of entertainment for people when they are stuck waiting somewhere, such as in line at a store or in the airport, since virtually everyone always has their mobile phone with them. It's not a surprise then that 12 of the top 25 most popular applications in the iTunes App Store are games, which are excellent diversions and can be stopped and started easily.

For example, the all-time number one downloaded application, Tapulous' Tap Tap Revenge (a Guitar Hero-like game), has been downloaded by nearly one-third of all iPhone/iPod Touch application users.[2] The key to Tap Tap Revenge's success is two-fold. One, it has compelling content: Guitar Hero meets Dance Dance Revolution. Also, Tapulous released a stripped-down free version to attract users, who then often downloaded the more extensive paid version (more on this in the Marketing Tactics section). The lessons to be drawn for political applications are clear: have compelling content that provides a welcome diversion, and give it away for free (and perhaps have a glitzier version available for contributors).

One size does not fit all: What works well on a carrier deck does not translate well to phones like the iPhone (and what's more, not all mobile phones are alike). On that same note, what is very successful on a website will not directly translate to success on a mobile application interface, or among different kinds of mobile interfaces. The reason for this is that users expect different things from different mediums. When they are on their phones instead of the computer, they expect a cleaner, quicker, to-the-point interface. Among different kinds of phones even, there may be a need for different design – when users have a touch screen, for example, they expect to touch to click. So a successful strategy is not to try to change users' expectations, but instead, to try to meet them (and even better – exceed them!). Equally importantly, a successful application will be different for the specific devices for which they are built.

Intuitive and Sleek Design: No surprise here, but looks can smooth over a lot. Mobile phone users are restricted to a very small and limiting screen, but that is no reason to design an application that looks and feel like it belongs in the dark ages. Each mobile phone and mobile operating system has different navigation tools and expected design elements. Know your audience and design to meet these expectations.

Make Your Goals Obvious: You cannot assume that users have the attention span to figure out what your application does and how it works. Therefore, strive to make your application instantly understandable to users. You can do this by minimizing the number of controls from which users have to choose and labeling functionality clearly so users immediately understand exactly what they do.

A Need for Speed: An application might be flashy and have all the bells and the whistles imaginable, but if it does not fully load before people's attention span is spent, it will not be successful (and in this fast-paced world, attention spans are getting shorter and shorter). Users expect applications to load quickly and perform without hiccups, so be sure to look at this when testing. If you do not meet this expectation, anticipate negative reviews on the app store (which sometimes can never be overcome) and for your mobile application to not meet your fundamental goals for building it (fundraising, GOTV, etc.).

Think Top Down: Mobile phone users scan their screens from top to bottom. Consequently, information displayed should cascade from broad to specific.

Keep it Short: Keep in mind, mobile users do not have the luxury of a large screen and are often looking for specific information while on the go. Therefore, identify the most important information, express it with few words, and display it prominently so users do not have to rummage through the application to find the thing for which they're looking.

Minimize Required Input: Whether users tap controls or use the keyboard, inputting information takes time and attention. Applications that require a lot of user input before anything useful happens can be off putting and frustrating.

Provide Fingertip-Size Targets: If you are designing for a touch screen phone, like the iPhone, it is important not to have the navigation controls (like buttons) too close together. A good mobile phone application design will space controls and other user-interaction elements sufficiently apart from one another so that users can tap accurately with a minimum of effort.

Successful Application Marketing Tactics

Don't Expect People to Spend Money for something they Have Not Seen: If your iPhone application is a paid application, also release a sized-down, free version to give users a taste of the experience. Most users, regardless of economic conditions, but even more so in a slow economy, are not willing to drop $4.99 on an application they have never seen. Some users will no doubt spend money on a concept (or, in our case, a candidate) without seeing the application. But the key to sustained, long-term success is getting past those early adopters/ supporters and free spenders and into a broader marketplace.

For example, when Ethan Nicholas, developer of the game application iShoot, launched his application, the first two days yielded high returns, but after that, downloads slid down and leveled off. In hopes of sparking sales, he released a free version without all of the bells and whistles of the original paid version. "It worked: iShoot Lite has been downloaded more than 2 million times, and many people have upgraded to the paid version."[3]

Early Success Yields Higher Returns: Momentum from the very beginning will help make your mobile application a success. To generate user interest before launch, build a website with information about the mobile application (collect email addresses, and notify the members of the list when the application is available), create a teaser web video that is either funny or compelling in some other way, and let people know when the application will be available through your existing communications channels (email, ads, etc.).

However, don't only focus on early success – sustained success requires continued marketing efforts. Once your mobile application is live, be sure to encourage early fans to write good reviews. Often times, reviews are only written when people are displeased. Reviews can make or break an application, so make sure your best face is put forward.

Cross-Promotion: Make sure your supporters are aware of your application; if they are not aware of it, they won't download it. You can do this by mentioning the mobile application at events, adding it to direct mail and email pieces, and noting it in your TV and online ads.

Submit the application to awards: Show off your hard work by submitting your application for awards. There are not many politicos doing mobile work, so your chances of winning are high and it's a great opportunity for earned media.

Advertising to Mobile Users via Mobile: Reach mobile users through their phones by placing targeted mobile advertising. Use networks like Quattro, Millennial Media, Third Screen Media, and AdMob. Often, these advertising networks will help you with targeting your ads and even with the creative elements if you ask.

If you don't have a budget for mobile advertising, consider alternatives such as AdMob's Download Exchange program: www.admob.com/exchange/. This program helps you create the graphics for your ad and then places it on like-minded applications also in the exchange program. It is essentially a new version of a link exchange program.

Obama '08 for iPhone

The point of this chapter is to get you thinking about how mobile phone applications can be used for more than just diversionary games; and instead can be used to influence people and to effect change. The 2008 presidential election cycle was the first time mobile phone applications have ever played a role in campaigning, and then-candidate Barack Obama used it particularly effectively. The Obama '08 for iPhone application was released in September 2008, with the goal of helping supporters become more directly involved with the campaign. It was offered for free, and created for free by volunteers, who developed it over 22 days.

The application is a great example of how mobile technology can tap into any campaign's core goal: reach people and either persuade them or get them active. The Obama '08 for iPhone application created "two-minute activists" by tapping into the user's address book, searching for contacts in battleground states, and suggesting the user call them. The "Call Your Friends" tool allowed users to write reminder notes to themselves regarding which friends they had already called, who those friends were supporting and who wanted a reminder call on Election Day. The application also allowed users to find the closest campaign office and gave directions from the location of the user at that moment, using the mapping function, making it easier for people to know where to go if they wanted to help.

Other Obama '08 for iPhone features included:

- Call Stats: See nationwide Obama '08 Call Friends totals and find out how your call totals compare to leading callers.
- Receive Updates: Receive the latest news and announcements via text messages or email.
- News: Browse complete coverage of national and local campaign news.
- Local Events: Find local events, share by email and get maps and directions.
- Media: Browse videos and photos from the campaign
- Issues: Get clear facts about Barack Obama and Joe Biden's plan for essential issues facing Americans.[4]

Final Thoughts

As you can see, mobile phone applications are still an emerging and developing field. While it can be scary to forge into unknown territory, remember that anything is possible; there is still room for new ideas, new developments, and new approaches. So if you are looking to be at the forefront of technology with your campaign, experiment with a mobile application. Success could yield interaction and mobilization from highly engaged supporters that would otherwise be dormant.

REFERENCES

[1] In-Stat Press Release, "Mobile Application Store Users to Quadruple in Five Years, Opening New Opportunities for Marketers,"
www.instat.com/press.asp?ID=2483&sku=IN0904424MCM

[2] comScore Press Release, "Tapulous's (sic) Tap Tap Revenge Has Been Downloaded by 1 out of 3 iTunes Application Users,"
www.comsore.com/press/release.asp?press=2768

[3] Wortham, Jenna, "The iPhone Gold Rush,"
www.nytimes.com/2009/04/05/fashion/05iphone.html?_r=1&scp=1&sq=The%20iPhone%20gold%20rush&st=cse

[4] Obama Website,
my.barackobama.com/page/content/iphone

PART IV
Building Community

CHAPTER 18

The New Face
of Activism

Karen A.B. Jagoda

The web is changing the face of activism. We are beginning to realize that persuasion can take many forms and voters are being persuaded in small ways that add up to a larger impression. Getting a constituent to open an email from a candidate, forward a message, sign up for a newsletter or contribute online are just some of the ways to simply engage a potential voter. There are also other activities going on that can influence voters in unpredictable ways.

The results from the E-Voter Institute 2008 survey of Voter Expectations reveal voters are more likely to use the Internet to research and view candidate materials and tell others about what they discover, than to pursue more active political actions such as donating or submitting an email address in order to receive information from a candidate.

Democrats are more likely to engage in online political activities than Republicans and Independents. Republicans report receiving more email from friends and family about politics and are slightly more inclined to forward links and email than Democrats.

The E-Voter Institute 2008 surveys of voters before and immediately after the election asked respondents to describe themselves in terms of how politically active they were and to indicate if they had voted. Clearly those who voted spent more time online searching for information, checking out the candidate web site and reading and forwarding email about campaign activities.

Over one quarter of those who did not vote still searched for information about candidates and nearly as many forwarded links or email to friends and family about politics and visited a candidate web site. Perhaps most surprisingly, 31% of those who did not vote watched online videos about candidates and 30% received emails from friends or family about politics. Is this an indication that politics and political campaigns might be seen as entertainment and not necessarily something that requires any real action like voting?

Looking at the same activities this time by level of political activism and political affiliation reveals how important it is to focus on a variety of ways for voters to become engaged with a campaign. There will always be people who simply vote based on a few bits of information about a candidate or ballot initiative but 25% those who do not consider themselves politically active still searched for information about a candidate, visited a candidate web site and slightly more watched online videos about a candidate. These people are active in a new way that needs to be recognized and capitalized on.

It is no surprise that the E-Voter Institute 2008 post election research revealed that those 18-24 years old showed the most interest in all things Internet, but they are the least likely to forward links and email to friends and family.

Those 25-34 years old are least likely to give up an email address in order to receive online information from candidates. About 50% of those 18-54 listen to online radio. Over 50% of each age category had visited a candidate's web site and those 65-74 years old showed a significant interest in viewing online video about a candidate.

Candidates and advocates who figure out how to encourage their supporters to forward email, watch online video and share links with friends and family will greatly enhance their field operations with little additional cost.

Political Actions Taken in 2008			
Political Actions	Voted at the poll	Voted absentee/ mail-in	Did not vote
Received email from friends or family about politics	58%	60%	30%
Searched online for additional information about politics	56%	58%	28%
Visited a candidate's web site	54%	57%	23%
Viewed online videos about candidates	54%	56%	31%
Told a friend or family to vote for a candidate or initiative	52%	57%	18%
Forwarded links or email to friends/family about political issues	47%	50%	23%
Read a blog about politics or candidates	40%	40%	21%
Participated in an online discussion about politics	31%	30%	14%
Submitted an email address in order to received candidate information	30%	36%	9%
Watched a webcast from a candidate event	29%	30%	18%
Sent an email to a candidate or politician about your concerns	27%	30%	8%
Clicked on an online political ad	26%	28%	13%
Donated to a candidate or cause online	17%	22%	3%
Attended a candidate event	13%	16%	3%
Volunteered for a political campaign	12%	14%	4%
Donated to a candidate or cause using a check or credit card in response to direct mail or to attend an event	10%	13%	2%

E-Voter Institute 2008 Post Election Survey of Voters

Political Actions Taken

Political Actions	Total	Level of Political Activism		
		Very Politically Active	Occasionally active in politics	Not active other than voting
Visited a candidate web site	41%	64%	52%	25%
Viewed online videos about candidates	40%	57%	48%	28%
Searched online for additional information about politics	38%	58%	48%	25%
Told a friend or family to vote for a candidate or initiative	34%	56%	43%	19%
Received email from friends or family about politics	33%	46%	39%	24%
Forwarded links or email to friends/family - political issues	28%	47%	34%	18%
Read a blog about politics or candidates	27%	48%	33%	16%
Sent an email to a candidate or politician about your concerns	22%	41%	27%	13%
Participated in an online discussion about politics	18%	42%	22%	8%
Clicked on an online political ad	18%	40%	21%	8%
Submitted an email address in order to received candidate information	17%	40%	22%	7%
Attended a political event	16%	39%	23%	4%
Donated to a candidate or cause online	13%	34%	16%	4%
Volunteered for a political campaign	9%	31%	12%	1%

E-Voter Institute 2008 Post Election Survey of Voters

Political Actions Taken in 2008 By Age

Political Actions	18-24	25-34	35-54	55-64	65-74	75+
Received email from friends or family about politics	46%	51%	56%	66%	76%	72%
Searched online for additional information about politics	58%	54%	53%	53%	54%	45%
Viewed online videos about candidates	55%	50%	51%	56%	59%	38%
Visited a candidate's web site	57%	52%	51%	54%	50%	31%
Told a friend or family to vote for a candidate or initiative	57%	50%	47%	51%	58%	41%
Forwarded links or email to friends/family about political issues	38%	42%	44%	54%	72%	62%
Read a blog about politics or candidates	46%	41%	37%	32%	38%	14%
Submitted an email address in order to received candidate information	34%	25%	29%	33%	39%	24%
Participated in an online discussion about politics	37%	29%	31%	21%	20%	14%
Watched a webcast from a candidate event	26%	26%	29%	30%	25%	17%
Sent an email to a candidate or politician about your concerns	20%	19%	28%	32%	51%	45%
Clicked on an online political ad	28%	23%	25%	28%	30%	14%
Donated to a candidate or cause online	17%	16%	16%	18%	27%	34%
Attended a candidate event	17%	11%	12%	14%	15%	7%
Volunteered for a political campaign	13%	11%	12%	12%	17%	10%
Donated to a candidate or cause using a check or credit card in response to direct mail or to attend an event	8%	7%	10%		17%	38%

E-Voter Institute 2008 Third Annual Survey of Voter Expectations

Political Actions Taken in 2008
Comparison Total Voters Pre and Post Election

Political Actions	Pre-Election	Post Election
Received email from friends or family about politics	33%	56%
Searched online for additional information about politics	38%	54%
Viewed online videos about candidates	40%	52%
Visited a candidate's web site	41%	52%
Told a friend or family to vote for a candidate or initiative	34%	49%
Forwarded links or email to friends/family about political issues	28%	45%
Read a blog about politics or candidates	27%	38%
Submitted an email address in order to received candidate information	17%	29%
Participated in an online discussion about politics	18%	29%
Sent an email to a candidate or politician about your concerns	22%	26%
Clicked on an online political ad	18%	25%
Donated to a candidate or cause online	13%	17%
Attended a candidate event	16%	13%
Volunteered for a political campaign	9%	12%
None of the above	21%	11%

E-Voter Institute 2008 Post Election Survey of Voters and E-Voter Institute 2008 Third Annual Survey of Voter Expectations

CHAPTER 19

Online Social Networks in Politics: Promise, Frustration and the Future

Colin Delany

Is 2008 the MySpace/Facebook election? You might think so from the political attention and resources invested in online social networks in the past year or so. The top presidential campaigns all amassed much-chronicled lists of hundreds of thousands of "friends" on MySpace and Facebook, and the Obama and McCain campaigns also invested in custom social networks for supporters early on (MyBarackObama has built to hundreds of thousands of members, while McCain's equivalent never hit critical mass and died when his overall campaign first imploded in the middle of 2007).

But for all the prominence of online social networks, they haven't been as critical to this year's primaries as some had predicted. On the other hand, from the Reverend Wright clips, to "Yes We Can," to "Bomb Bomb Iran," online video has been significant in shaping the race, at times even altering the fundamental direction of a campaign. As for direct supporter communications, candidates are still more likely to send email to donors and volunteers than to use social networking sites to reach them.

Instead of social networking, the online technology that's really shaken up 2008 is fundraising. The candidates' ability to raise almost unlimited amounts of money online has been a true game-changer, allowing Barack Obama to opt out of public financing and to begin to build a significant Democratic financial advantage for the first time in political memory.

The Promise

Yet the data in the 2008 E-Voter Institute study show that online social networks SHOULD be fertile ground for political organizers for by just about any measure, users of websites such as MySpace, Facebook and LinkedIn are more likely to be politically active than average citizens. For instance, they're more likely to donate to a candidate, more likely to join a political email list, more likely to visit a candidate's site, more likely to click on a candidate's ad -- in fact, they're more likely to mention even RECEIVING political email from a friend or family member, which suggests a high degree of back-and-forth interaction about politics in their online (and probably offline) lives.

Significantly, the trend toward relatively high levels of political interest and activity holds true beyond just the top social network enthusiasts. In most cases, average MySpace/Facebook users were closer in behavior to the technically advanced social networkers than they were to people who are not members of a social network. For whatever reason, online social networks seem to attract a disproportionate number of politically active people. (Wild conjecture: I suspect that it has both to do with the relatively young age of social networking site users in a year in which the darn kids are politically active, as well as with the natural tendency of all social spaces to attract people who are in general directed outward into the public sphere.)

The Frustration

As plenty of activists in the nonprofit and political advocacy worlds have found, using online social networks for political outreach can be extremely time-consuming. The results in terms of supporters gained, funds raised or advocacy actions taken are at times astonishing, but in many other cases they're not -- they're often no more than comparable with those gained from email list-building and other forms of online outreach, and are frequently worse. A similar situation seems to exist on the electoral side: the presidential campaigns certainly use online social networking sites, but they drive most fundraising and local organizing via email and they capture most supporters directly through their own websites.

Why the divide? If social networkers are so politically active, why haven't Facebook and MySpace come to dominate the ways campaigns find, organize and mobilize supporters online? Once again, the E-Voter Survey suggests some reasons.

My Space, Indeed

The most critical E-Voter 2008 data are in responses to the questions: "How do you expect candidates to use the Internet?" and "What are the best ways for a candidate or advocate to get your attention for the 2008 election?" In both cases, those surveyed put social networking outreach near the bottom of the list overall: only 38% expected candidates to use online social networks, vs. 60% expecting online video and 70% online fundraising. As for getting voters' attention, only 36% of hard-core MySpace and Facebook enthusiasts listed social networking sites as a top way to reach them, comparable with direct mail and only a hair above newspaper and radio advertising!

Why? I suspect that one big reason lies in the very nature of online social networking. People have a sense that these sites aren't broadcast tools, that they are indeed actual social networks. Most members limit who can see details of their lives, and except for the obsessive "friend" collectors among us, most limit their networks largely to people they actually know.

In other words, MySpace may be too aptly named for its own financial good: each page is indeed "my space" to its owner and user, and many resist intrusions on their profiles, by ignoring commercial entreaties and overwhelming paid advertising with their own installed games, videos, music and custom layouts.

Note that this "problem" -- to me it sounds like a healthy response -- doesn't just exist for political marketers, since if it were easy to find paying customers for commercial products on social networking sites, Facebook would have earned more than $150 million off of advertising to its umpteen million users last year.

Reaching the Networked

I suspect that the most effective solutions for reaching voters via MySpace and Facebook will use the sites' strengths by treating them as actual webs of connections rather than as broadcast tools. They'll derive their power from the fact that individual links between users generally do reflect real social relationships, and that we give communications from trusted sources disproportionate weight. As some in the online advocacy field have found, if real people do real outreach through real social connections, the results can be amazing -- but often at a great cost in time. As online organizer Ivan Boothe wrote recently about his work with the Genocide Intervention Network,

"We're not simply looking for a mailing list or an ATM -- we want an educated, active movement of people interested in preventing and stopping genocide. Our members need to be able to think for themselves on the issue -- to hold events in their communities, motivate others to take action, press their elected representatives to take [a] stand -- not to simply be another name on a list, but to be a hub in an ever-expanding network."

Which is pretty far from being a one-to-many mass-communications operation: we're talking about working closely (and frequently one-on-one) with people on Facebook and similar sites over a long period of time to help build a cadre of very committed activists, something that most electoral campaigns simply can't do, because of a lack of time, money, staff or all of the above.

That being said, whether or not campaigns have the resources for in-depth social networking outreach, it's becoming painfully easy to provide basic tools to followers that let them spread the word FOR you. Campaign profile pages are free, for starters, and more and more of the standard political-world web-hosting tools are providing options (from widgets to badges to petitions) that allow campaigns to encourage supporters to become evangelists on blogs, discussion groups -- AND social networking sites.

Citizen activism is something that we've seen an explosion of in this cycle, much of it welcomed by candidates ("Yes We Can"), some of it not ("FWD: barack hussein obama is a secret muslim intent on overthrowing the government from within"). Individual citizens' use of email, Facebook, MySpace, YouTube, Twitter and every other online tool to promote their causes and candidates has exploded, and campaigns will ignore the real potential of citizen activists (including your email-forwarding uncle -- see the results of E-Voter Survey) at their own peril. Most will find it better to try to harness the beast than to live entirely at its mercy.

Plus, more-traditional mass outreach may still work in online social settings, since extensive advertising on MySpace, Facebook and LinkedIn is still relatively untested, and campaigns with the resources to buy ads targeted at their particular electoral districts may find them an effective way to tap a politically active audience. Once converted by whatever means, each site user is a potential advocate for a campaign in any communications channel he or she uses, online or off.

The Future

Some enthusiasts believe that within a few years we'll all be enveloped in a weave of online social networks from waking until dark, and in that case, online communications strategies will no doubt change. My suspicion is that social networking sites will continue to be a significant part of people's online lives, with most professionals at least having the equivalent of a LinkedIn or Facebook page, for instance. A much smaller number of us will invest big chunks of our online selves on the equivalent of profile pages, but I suspect that this will still represent a sizeable and disproportionately political (and hence valuable) audience.

And as television commercials and other mass-audience channels steadily lose effectiveness, campaigns may NEED the potential evangelists that social networking sites naturally draw in -- building an army of active and aggressive supporters may be the only way to cut through the endless clutter of media saturation and reach actual voters. But, that's a story for another day.

CHAPTER 20

Influencing Social Network Members

Karen A.B. Jagoda

E-Voter Institute 2008 research revealed that social network members are less influenced by television and more influenced by Internet information than the general voter. Active social net members are 75% more likely than non-members and 33% more likely than all voters to be influenced by Internet information.

There is remarkable consistency across all categories of social network membership when evaluating how voters make decisions. Only when we look at social network membership by party affiliation do we see distinct differences in influences, with Republicans nearly twice as likely to vote for the family favorite and Democrats clearly favoring television.

			Member	
		Member	Does Not	
	Total	Frequently	Frequently	Non
Influence	Voters	Updates	Update	Member
Most Effect on Voting Decision By Social Network Status				
Television	34%	30%	31%	37%
Internet information	21%	28%	26%	16%
Who my family votes for	7%	7%	7%	7%
Newspaper editorials	6%	5%	5%	7%
Recommendations from my political party	5%	6%	6%	5%
Friends	5%	6%	4%	5%
Endorsements	3%	3%	2%	3%
Direct mail	2%	2%	1%	3%
Phone calls from campaign volunteers	0%	1%	0%	0%

E-Voter Institute 2008 Third Annual Survey of Voter Expectations

Activities of Social Net Members

E-Voter Institute 2008 research showed that active social network members, compared to non-members, are nearly 4 times more likely to post to blogs and use widgets, more than twice as likely to post ratings and comments, and seven times more likely to have their own blog.

Active social network members are clearly more active across a wide range of Internet activities than the average voter and non- members of social networks. Those who are not as active but still members of a social net are 24% more likely to make online purchases than active social net users. Maybe they have more time because they are not concentrating on their social net updates.

Most Effect in Voting Decision
By Social Net Membership and Party Affiliation

Influences	Total Members			Non Members		
	Dem	Rep	Ind	Dem	Rep	Ind
Television	34%	27%	29%	41%	33%	34%
Internet information	27%	25%	29%	15%	15%	20%
Recommendations from my political party	7%	10%	3%	5%	8%	2%
Who my family votes for	6%	10%	6%	6%	10%	4%
Newspaper editorials	6%	4%	7%	7%	7%	7%
Friends	4%	4%	4%	5%	4%	5%
Endorsements	2%	2%	3%	4%	3%	3%
Direct mail	1%	1%	2%	2%	3%	2%
Phone calls from campaign volunteers	0%	0%	0%	1%	0%	0%

E-Voter Institute 2008 Third Annual Survey of Voter Expectations

Online Activity	Total	Member Frequently Updates	Member Does Not Frequently Update	Non Member
Characteristics of Voters By Social Network Status				
Use email	92%	95%	97%	89%
Make online purchases	79%	85%	89%	72%
Have broadband access to the Internet at home	73%	84%	84%	65%
Forward links and email to friends/family	69%	80%	80%	60%
Read newspapers or magazines online	66%	81%	77%	57%
Play online games	57%	73%	68%	47%
Download video and/or audio	53%	75%	70%	39%
Have wireless capability	53%	73%	63%	42%
Post ratings or comments online	46%	73%	62%	31%
Listen to online radio	44%	63%	52%	35%
Social network member	44%	100%	100%	0%
Upload video and/or audio	33%	61%	43%	21%
Post to other blogs	28%	57%	41%	15%
Use widgets	19%	40%	25%	10%
Maintain a blog or your own web site	19%	49%	27%	7%
Subscribe to RSS feeds	18%	36%	24%	10%
Use Twitter or other micro-blogging sites	5%	20%	6%	2%

E-Voter Institute 2008 Third Annual Survey of Voter Expectations

2008: A Year of Significant Change for Online Communities

The E-Voter Institute 2008 post election survey of voters revealed that social network members experienced some significant changes in their behavior with those using Twitter jumping from 5% to 14% between May and November. Across all respondents, usage of Twitter and other micro-blogging sites rose from 5% to 9% with big jumps in those 18-54 years old.

The survey also revealed a big jump in the use of Facebook among social network members from 55% to 72%, with those 55-64 years old showing a dramatic jump from 41% to 65% and those 65+ realizing they need to get involved, showing an unexpected jump from 20%-55% participating.

There was a significant jump in Facebook usage among those social network members who called themselves competent computer users in addition to the self-described advanced and power users. Likewise, LinkedIn usage jumped from 15% to 21% between May and November 2008 among social network members.

Membership in Social Networks Pre and Post Election 2008		Total
Social Net	May-08	Nov-08
Facebook	55%	72%
MySpace	76%	70%
LinkedIn	15%	21%
Twitter	5%	14%
Digg	8%	12%
Live Journal	11%	11%
Other	11%	10%
Eventful	2%	3%

E-Voter Institute 2008 Post Election Survey of Voters and the E-Voter Institute 2008 Third Annual Survey of Voter Expectations

Membership in Social Networks By Pre-/Post Election and Age									
	18-24		25-34		35-54		55-64		65-74	
Social Net	Pre	Post	Pre	Post	Pre	Post	Pre	Post	Pre	Post
Facebook	85%	88%	59%	76%	44%	64%	41%	65%	20%	55%
MySpace	65%	65%	80%	72%	77%	72%	66%	63%	87%	55%
LinkedIn	9%	12%	18%	24%	15%	22%	13%	22%	0%	23%
Twitter	5%	14%	6%	15%	5%	16%	6%	6%	0%	9%
Digg	9%	14%	10%	15%	6%	11%	10%	7%	0%	5%
Live Journal	15%	18%	13%	13%	9%	9%	5%	8%	0%	0%
Other	5%	7%	7%	7%	14%	11%	22%	18%	20%	32%
Eventful	2%	7%	4%	4%	2%	2%	0%	0%	0%	0%

E-Voter Institute 2008 Post Election Survey of Voters and the E-Voter Institute 2008 Third Annual Survey of Voter Expectations

---

From the Spot-on Weekly Spotlight June 22, 2009

50,000,000 Facebook Fans Can't Be Wrong

But They Need Something To Do

There's no doubt that in the political campaign world, Facebook is the Bright Shiny Thing everyone's got their eyes on, especially since a first-term Senator from Illinois won the presidency last year. But all this activity triggers a question that doesn't have an easy answer: How many campaigns are actually using Facebook effectively, and how many are just wasting their time?

Case Study: The Race to Get Lots of "Friends" and "Fans" on Facebook. If you're on Facebook for more than 5 minutes, you know how easy it is to passively express affinity for anyone, or anything. Maybe you see a friend has become a "fan" of (fill in the blank) "Bacon" or "Not Being on Fire," or maybe Rush Limbaugh and Batman. With a couple of clicks of the mouse, you join the bandwagon. It's fun, and it's a social "me-too" function that's an integral part of Facebook.

After Barack Obama's much-publicized efforts to collect Facebook friends, politicians and their advisors have jumped on this. Now it's common to see candidates for office engage in a "friend recruitment war," sending out repeated pleas to their supporters to "get more friends" for them, and to hit some magic target. As this desperate struggle for "more friends" continues, politicians risk looking less like capable leaders in difficult times, and more like insecure teenagers running for Homecoming King or Queen instead. Having a lot of friends can be great but often it's no different than having 5,000 or 10,000 yard signs – all sitting on your front yard, not distributed throughout the neighborhood.

Drives to "get more friends and fans" on Facebook miss the potential power of social networking for campaigns as a field organizing tool, not a popularity contest. Obama's efforts on Facebook were part of a larger effort that combined online field work – on and off Facebook – and took advantage of the medium's novelty. Today, when Facebook is larger and more established, it's much less important if a politician has thousands of "fans" on Facebook. That's particularly true if none of them do anything offline to help out the campaign effort. Or if campaigns don't know anything about their "fans" or "friends."

If a campaign only has a few hundred "fans," with every one of those fans knocking on doors in their hometown, raising money, and telling their friends - on and offline - about the campaign, the candidate will be doing a lot better where it really counts - at the polls on Election Day. Consultants who want to help their clients the most need to look at social networking not as a gimmick, bolted on to a traditional campaign plan, but instead as an extension of their field plan, just done online. Using Facebook's many tools to identify, recruit and organize supporters online , and giving them something meaningful to *do*, will ensure that their campaigns are more successful than the insecure teenager begging for more friends.

CHAPTER 21

2012-The Perfect Online Storm: The User-Generated Tsunami is Coming

Kevin O'Neill

The 2008 election at last brought America the "Internet election," that pundits and consultants heralded since 1996. After every cycle the question that was always asked was, "What is the role of the Internet in politics?" The unequivocal answer now is that the roles of Internet and technology will be to rapidly evolve political communications, just as it is quickly changing other aspects of society.

The dramatic changes caused by technology are most evident by looking at the end of the 2004 election. At the time, Facebook was only 10 months old, John Kerry raised the most money online with $82 million[1], and the first YouTube video[2] was still 171 days away from being uploaded and now a little more than four years later, there's now 225 million Facebook members worldwide, Barack Obama raised $500 million online[3], and there are 5 *billion* of Youtube videos viewed *in a month*[4].

During this past election, many political web videos were virally spread through email and social networking, and then further amplified by mainstream news. While voter-generated messages like JibJab were widely seen in the 2004 election, the frequency and breadth of web videos in 2008 established online video as a viable channel for political participation. Additionally, the most viral content was not always generated by the campaigns. Videos like "Yes We Can" and the footage of Rev. Wright's sermons exhibited the positive and negative impact on a campaign that videos distributed by the electorate can have.

In 2008, voter-generated content was not limited to videos, as it was also produced through a myriad of other online channels including millions of blog posts and comments, tweets, Facebook status updates, photos and even t-shirt designs on CafePress. All the content produced in this past election will only be a fraction of what will surface from the electorate in the next cycle, just as online fundraising totals in 2004 were dwarfed by the staggering figures raised online in 2008.

The Forecast for 2012

Making an accurate technological forecast for the 2012 presidential race is challenging as there are innovations yet to emerge on the horizon, but there are remarkable trends converging which point to an unprecedented surge in content generated and consumed by voters. This rise will be fueled by more homes and phones with faster Internet speeds, more social networking that increases content distribution and creation, the lowering of video production barriers and the allure to produce content for an increasing larger audience.

These trends will spur an online "perfect storm" that will unleash the online expression of the electorate in unprecedented speed, magnitude, and scope fueling a deluge of voter-generated messages that will overwhelm the campaigns, the traditional media, and the electorate.

A Larger Audience and More Content Creators

The 2008 election was sprinkled with voter-generated content in the form of election-focused web videos, dozens of which received nationwide coverage out of the hundreds of thousands that were produced.

By 2012, content created by voters will flood the political landscape, as the number of creators of user-generated content is estimated by eMarketer to increase by 30% from 2008, and the number of creators of user-generated video alone will jump by 62%. The audience for user-generated content will grow by 29% from 2008 to 2012.

User-generated content creators (which includes political content) are defined by eMarketer as individuals who create and share online, any of the following media at least once per month: video, audio, photos, personal blogs, personal Web sites, online bulletin board postings, customer reviews or personal profiles in social networks or virtual worlds. By the same token, user-generated content consumers are those who consume any of those media types in the same time frame.

US User-Generated Content Creator by Content Type (millions)			
	2008	2012	Change
User Generated Video	15.4	24.9	62%+
Social Networking	71.3	100.1	40%+
Blogs	21.2	30.2	43%+
UGC Creators	82.5	108	30%+

US User-Generated Content Consumers (Millions and % of Internet users)		
2008	2012	Change
100.8 (52%)	130.12 (60%)	29+

The Growth of Social Networking

In 2008, social networks helped fuel the creation and sharing of voter-generated content such as videos, photos, comments and status updates. The political impact of social networking will grow dramatically as more of the electorate uses these sites. The number of Americans using social networks will increase by 44% to 115 million in 2013 up from 79 million in 2008[5].

More social networking within the electorate will not only allow content to spread more easily, but it will be more rewarding in 2012 for creators as their content may likely be seen by more people.

The Increase of Internet Broadband

When America was gearing up for the primaries in 2007, 54% of households had a broadband Internet connection, but by 2012, that will increase to 77% of U.S. households[6]. This jump will expand the amount of content consumed and produced as broadband allows users to upload and download large amounts of video.

Cisco, the company that makes servers and routers that manage broadband Internet traffic, predicts that from 2008 to 2012, that traffic associated with commercial video content will *quintuple*, and traffic from user-generated video will *triple*[7]. The amount of data associated with Internet video in 2012 will be nearly 400 times the size of the entire U.S. Internet backbone in 2000[8]. Online video will certainly be a growing driver of bandwidth usage.

The Voter is the "New" Media Consultant

Before 2008, media consultants, campaign staff, and news organizations largely generated all video messaging related to a campaign. The last election changed that, and the rise of political web videos produced by voters will be dramatically amplified in 2012 as improvements in video hardware and software are lowering the barriers to video production, and more voters will have the tools to edit, shoot, and distribute (Hoge) online videos.

One of the most recent innovations in video capture technology is the Flip Camera, a video camcorder the size of a phone which takes up to one hour of HD quality video and shares it through a USB connector, enabling the user upload the content to the computer, email it, and share it to sites like YouTube and MySpace. More than two million Flip cameras were sold since its debut in September 2007, beating every company outside of Sony.

In March 2009, Cisco purchased Pure Digital, the company that makes the Flip camera. This acquisition is in line with Cisco's outlook that Internet traffic will be driven by the growth of video and visual networking. In an interview with CNET.com about the sale a Cisco executive said, *"Today, Flip Video camcorders use the PC to get to the Internet...but every product will be directly connected to the Internet."*[9] The instant transfer of longer, high quality videos from anywhere to the Internet on a mass scale (beyond early adopters) will certainly make an impact in the amount of user-generated content related to elections.

With the increased demand to produce video, more sophisticated video production software is becoming free or more affordable. The last week of the 2008 election, Google released Picasa 3, their free photo editing and organizing software with a basic Movie Maker suite with an option to upload directly to YouTube. Picasa and other free video production tools like Adobe's Remix and Jumpcut.com will become increasingly sophisticated and higher-end products, like Final Cut Pro, may become affordable to meet the needs of the growing market of voter video producers.

The Mobile Web Video Explosion – Putting Politics in People's Pockets

The single most widespread technological advance that will impact the electorate will be the emergence of 4G (4th Generation) wireless networks. Presently, most cell phones in the United States are on 2G and 3G networks (like the Iphone), which can reach speeds around 1 Mbps (megabytes per second).

4G-enabled devices will be widely available during the next election, as a new 4G standard called LTE (Long Term Evolution), will be deployed initially by Verizon Wireless beginning in select cities in 2010, with nationwide rollouts complete around 2013 or early 2014[10]. Overall, 4G adoption is expected to adopted more quickly than 3G, as it is predicted to have 100 million subscribers in four years, while that milestone took six years for 3G.[11]

Initial speed tests of 4G are presently clocking data transfers at a blazing 60-100 mbps, but the battery life of wireless devices will not be able to sustain so much data activity, so the likely reality is that 4G speeds may be up to 8-12 mbps, which is far greater than even present-day broadband networks at 2-6 mbps. Mobile broadband may replace fixed broadband in some areas.[12]

These speeds will bring voters an upgraded user experience on their mobile devices, as 4G will enable streaming high-definition video, massive uploading and downloading of videos, and mobile video teleconferencing between candidates, staff, and volunteers. This next level of mobile speed will spur on more sophisticated mobile applications that enable voters to produce, capture, publish, and share content as they would on their home computers.

As 4G adoption grows and more voters have data plans, text messaging may decline in some markets, as voters may prefer not to pay "standard text messaging rates" when they can more deeply engage with their friends on their mobile device through social networking, instant messaging, video teleconferencing or email.

The emergence of 4G will contribute to political participation being able to be instantly captured, edited, uploaded and shared at anytime and from anywhere. The quality and amount of real time mobile content injected into the next presidential race will truly revolutionize how content is consumed and created online.

A Storm is Brewing...
Will Candidates Sink or Swim?

This forecast for the 2012 election season is foreboding for any candidate, but the campaign that is best prepared for these seismic technological shifts, will weather the storm, and be buoyed by the inundation of user-generated content.

For decades, campaigns have asked supporters to mobilize, donate, and vote, but they will need to ask them to frequently create and share content. By the next cycle, media will be further fragmented, making it that much more important for campaigns to strategically drive their supporters to produce and distribute voter-generated content.

If campaigns choose to ignore this upcoming sea change messages, then rogue waves of voter-produced messages may sideline their campaign and drown their messaging at levels unseen in 2008.

Fueled by changing technological winds, the 2012 election season will be flooded with a tsunami of content from the electorate that will send unparalleled shockwaves throughout traditional political communications, and in its aftermath future president candidates will be even more beholden to the whims of the electorate.

REFERENCES

[1] Nathan Shaver, Highlights from the 2nd Annual Summit on Philanthropy, 10 29 2004, 18 April 2009
www.onphilanthropy.com/site/News2?page=NewsArticle&id=5882

[2] jawed, Me at the zoo, 23 April 2005, 18 May 2009
www.youtube.com/watch?v=jNQXAC9IVRw

[3] Jose Antonio Vargas, Obama Raised Half a Billion Online, 20 November 2008, 16 April 2009
voices.washingtonpost.com/44/2008/11/20/obama_raised_half_a_billion_on.html

[4] Nielsen, March Video Streaming Soars Nearly 40% Compared To Last Year, 13 April 2009, 3 May 2009
blog.nielsen.com/nielsenwire/online_mobile/march-video-streaming-soars-nearly-40-compared-to-last-year/

[5] Mark Walsh, eMarketer: U.S. Social Network Users To Grow 44% By 2013, 17 February 2009, 15 Paril 2009
www.mediapost.com/publications/?fa=Articles.showArticle&art_aid=100485

[6] Gartner, Gartner Says 17 Countries to Surpass 60 Percent Broadband Penetration into the Home by 2012, 24 July 2008, 18 April 2009
www.gartner.com/it/page.jsp?id=729907

[7] Cisco, Cisco Visual Networking Index: 2008 Year in Review / Video Highlights, 8 December 2008, 11 April 2009
www.cisco.com/en/US/solutions/collateral/ns341/ns525/ns537/ns705/ns827/white_paper_cll-512048.html

[8] Cisco, Approaching the Zetabyte Era, 16 June 2008, 7 April 2009
www.cisco.com/en/US/solutions/collateral/ns341/ns525/ns537/ns705/ns827/white_paper_cll-481374_ns827_Networking_Solutions_White_Paper.html

[9] Marguerite Reardon, Cisco buys Flip Video maker for $590 million, 19 March 2009, 20 March 2009
news.cnet.com/8301-1023_3-10199960-93.html

[10] Sascha Segan, Verizon Wireless Sharpens LTE Roadmap, 14 May 2009, 21 May 2009
www.pcmag.com/article2/0,2817,2347071,00.asp

[11] Marin Perez, 4G Wireless Growth Expected To Outpace 3G, 18 May 2009, 23 May 2009
www.informationweek.com/news/mobility/3G/showArticle.jhtml?articleID=217500667&subSection=News

[12] Cisco, Approaching the Zetabyte Era, 16 June 2008, 7 April 2009
www.cisco.com/en/US/solutions/collateral/ns341/ns525/ns537/ns705/ns827/white_paper_cll-481374_ns827_Networking_Solutions_White_Paper.html

E-Voter Institute Spotlight on
Consultants Who Miss the Impact of Online Video

E-Voter Institute 2008 research revealed that consultants still misinterpret signals from voters. These political consultants tend to over-estimate the effectiveness of online contribution appeals and the willingness of people to submit their email for updated candidate information.

While 54% of active social members view online video about candidates, only 7% of consultants think online video is effective for reaching the loyal base and 11% think online video is effective for reaching swing, Independent and undecided voters.

Even people who are not members of a social net are three times as likely to view online video about candidates as the consultants predict would be interested.

	Voters			Consultants	
Political Activity	**Total Voters**	**Member Updates Often**	**Non Member**	**Effective to reach Loyal base**	**Effective to Reach Other Voters**
Visited a candidate web site	41%	57%	32%	25%	22%
Viewed online videos about candidates	40%	54%	32%	7%	11%
Read a blog about politics or candidates	27%	42%	18%	8%	4%
Clicked on an online political ad	18%	32%	13%	5%	11%
Submitted an email address in order to received candidate information	17%	26%	12%	46%	13%

Voter Behavior and Consultants View of Effectiveness — Voters By Social Network Activity

E-Voter Institute 2008 Third Annual Survey of Voter Expectations and Seventh Annual Survey of Political and Advocacy Communications Leaders

CHAPTER 22

Wisdom of
the Crowds

Porter Bayne

With organized and self-organizing groups making big news and a big impact in the 2008 elections, most visibly with the campaigns for Barack Obama and Ron Paul, there is great, appropriate interest in understanding what "sourcing a crowd" means and how to do it to best assist campaign objectives. Crowdsourcing in a political campaign is an important, complex, and at times delicate interaction between a campaign and the rest of its community. What follows are a few definitions and observations to help guide those looking to gain from, and provide benefit to, the crowd in the course of an election cycle, from the perspective of an online tech guy.

What exactly is "crowdsourcing"? My favorite definition comes from the crowdsourced Wiktionary.org: "delegating a task to a large diffuse group, usually without monetary compensation". You've probably been participating in a crowdsourced task since you turned eighteen - the selection of elected officials in government.

Crowdsourcing has some key benefits in the context of a campaign:

1. Increase trust and participation from your supporters
    discover

2. Discover ideas and information you wouldn't otherwise
3. Reduce costs, financial and otherwise, on your campaign staff, by enabling volunteers to do simple tasks en masse
4. Get more bang for your buck from campaign actions

In addition to filling out campaign coffers via small donations and producing great videos of your opponent bumbling at a rally, truly powerful things can happen. Take 2008's Twitter Voter Report, where voters sent "tweets", identified with a unique label format that described any polling station around the country, reporting on conditions like how long the line was, perceived procedural problems, weather, and more. A Google map was dynamically populated with information, and you had an instant, organic collection of data that helped inform others on where and when to try and vote on Election Day. This is huge. No single organization could have (or would have) funded or coordinated this endeavor, but by having systems open to many - like Twitter - and a labeling system that was easy to understand, almost anyone could contribute, and concerned organizations were able to help spread the word to involve interested individuals.

Campaign 2008 saw some very innovative online endeavors in getting the public to help accomplish certain tasks and in some important cases, help identify which tasks to actually pursue.

Some exciting and interactive examples:

Apps for Democracy: (www.appsfordemocracy.org/. An effort in the District of Columbia, this effort invited developers to mix and match publicly available data and community input to produce useful online tools. Which was best? The crowd says: a DC carpool matchmaker.

Where for art thou, Robocaller?: Remember all the flap about misleading and unwanted robocalls during the campaign? Google Maps+ User Input= a very helpful map showing exactly which areas were targeted by which messages. www.epolitics.com/2008/10/30/tracking-political-robocalls-via-crowdsourcing-and-google-maps/.

Guns 'n Religion: Distributed, self-organized information collection is what caught President Obama in a controversial comment on guns and religion, and the struggling economies of middle America during the primaries.

Patriot Pact: When former Google engineer Vijay Boyapati volunteered to support the Ron Paul campaign, among the many successful efforts he and his cohorts spearheaded was a site for Paul supporters in New Hampshire to connect and stay at each other's homes as they canvassed and campaigned for the primary. www.nolanchart.com/article284.html.

Successfully crowdsource to build community and accomplish your goals

This is my definition, pieced together from a variety of smarter, preceding, and (with great apologies) uncited sources: *Give people a place and a way to help in the ways they want to help, more or less on their timeframe, in a way that connects them to others, encourages quality participation (as the crowd defines it!), rewards individual participation, and above all demonstrates the **impact** of the actions and output of the crowd.*

The key to participation is a sense of meaningful interaction: so a person feels that their contribution was heard or seen, and it helped.

Many tasks can and often should be crowdsourced - finding out what's being discussed in your community, disseminating information, executing a calling campaign, deciding which slogan to print on shirts, raising money, uploading and finding that essential rally photo or cell phone audio clip, and so on. If one person taking one action can be done cheaply, and adding all those cheap actions up amounts to something useful, crowdsource it.

(It's important to note that individuals connecting and befriending each other is crucial to community but not to crowdsourcing, and will introduce social pressures that may skew the results of a crowdsourced task. For example, I might prefer Jane's photo submission but Jim is my best friend, so I'll vote for his. Conversely, these social affiliations can help get things done - licking envelopes alone stinks, but with friends, it might just be *fun*. And a paper cut amongst my peers ain't so bad, and I probably won't whine much about it, either. This is a crucial tension to consider.)

Since you're trying to win a campaign and that includes building a community, let's look at the definition again. Both parts are key - the group is diffuse, or, made up of individuals acting generally on their own time and motives, and there isn't usually monetary compensation.

The first part matters because each person knows, for example, when, where and how they can best cast that vote for a candidate, issue, or a t-shirt slogan. People acting on their own time and motives doesn't mean they can't work together, it just means you're better off enabling, not dictating, their participation. It also means they are more likely to be satisfied with participating. If I love uploading and rating photos, and you need the best ten out of 1,000 rally photos selected, then enable me to do that. Don't first ask me to call and canvass voters. (If I'm having fun rating photos, maybe I'll canvass, too.) You may then see three of us self-organize a contest to get more photos when the first 1,000 were too blurry.

The second part matters, especially in advocacy and politics, because once you start paying or charging for participation, an individual becomes less collaborative and interested in teamwork, and instead begins placing a price on their input and that price is probably higher than you can pay.[1] People want to build the world they want to live in so long as they feel ownership in that world. Social rewards, which might include a pizza dinner for volunteers, or a "I helped the cause!" badge on their social networking profile, or the simple and undeniable satisfaction of rating someone else's content, are more appropriate for your *cause*. For more, see "The Cost of Social Norms". bookoutlines. pbwiki.com/Predictably-Irrational.

The primary challenges, then, are building and then maintaining the crowd that will help accomplish certain objectives.

Building the crowd. Finding the crowd. Empowering the crowd.

I think a community is a group of people whose interactions impact each other, even if they don't interact directly. I may not be very active, but my vote, my tweet, and my photo upload impact the community, as does yours. We might become friends, or we might not know each other exist.

As Clay Shirky notes in his important essay on groups and social software, *A Group Is Its Own Worst Enemy*[1], people that come together have some shared thing - an idea, a cause, some property, YOU - that they want to build and protect. This is the key. They feel ownership in this. (Consequently, they'll likely galvanize around a common enemy, too.) www.shirky.com/writings/group_enemy.html

To build the crowd online, enable flexible, interactive participation, and *build trust* amongst participants. Don't forget: you, too, are (also? merely?) a participant.

To that end, consider these:

1. Find someone experienced to help, hire, or point you in the right direction.
2. Create a common space (a site) where the crowd can meet.

3. What you build into a site impacts what people can do, so consider the features you add. If you want as many people possible to rate their favorite photo and give you an email address, give them a short form and a simple ratings system, don't require a comment, and don't ask them how old they are or where they live.

4. Participate, authentically, in the common space. This will grow your membership. Show the crowd, your community, that you are thoughtfully paying attention and responding. People prefer to listen to those they think are listening!

5. Consider a "constitution" or set of intentions and ground rules that

6. Inform the community you are trying to build. This is a powerful organizing principle that members will own. Every successful country has one.

7. Identify your core participants, get to know them, solicit their input, and empower them on your site. They will find more reasons to get involved.

8. Identity matters (an email address and nickname are usually fine). Anonymity makes it easy to be abusive, or simply not truly engage, within the common space.

9. Moderate to some degree. Allow the crowd to identify or even remove junk, spam, and offensive content. Some barriers to entry are good so that people see participation is valued.

10. Acknowledge contributions, and more importantly, enable members to acknowledge each others' contributions.

11. Train and demonstrate. You, your staff, and your
    core members can show others various ways to
    participate.

And of course, find pre-existing groups with aligned interests that you
can work with. A community that already trusts itself, and knows what
it is good at, is easier to mobilize then one that does not yet exist or is
still crystallizing.

Be more than just an email collection and blasting operation. Your
supporters are getting hit up constantly for attention and money; to get
their attention, you need to give them yours. And above all, if you ask
for the crowd's input, don't ignore it. This destroys hard-built trust.

People like to help, though they have limited time and interest. Most
want at least a little recognition for it from friends and notable members
of the community. And above all, we want to see the person or cause we
care about prevail.

Enable this to happen.

Groupthink vs. Crowdsourcing

In the debate between whether crowdsourcing means "wisdom of
the crowds" or "mob rule", the answer is "yes". What's the difference
between good crowdsourcing and groupthink?

Groupthink is "a type of thought exhibited by group members who
try to minimize conflict and reach consensus without critically testing,
analyzing, and evaluating ideas. (en.wikipedia.org/wiki/Groupthink)

In groupthink, group cohesion is so important that deviance is deterred
or punished.

To combat groupthink, it's best for there to be some individual incentive
to excel. A certain amount of anonymity can also combat groupthink,
though it must be balanced with identity as a tool for encouraging
accountability.

A group of people sharing an opinion is not necessarily groupthink.

Groupthink is a methodology for how someone came to an opinion, not the simple fact that people happen to share the same opinion.

Crowdsourcing isn't new to the web, but the web makes it a lot cheaper and generally easier to source a crowd. Doing it online is certainly not specific to politics either--businesses and research communities have been at it for years. It's simply because communication--the core of crowdsourcing--to the whole group, and amongst members within a group, is just easier and cheaper online.

PART V
Online Tools

CHAPTER 23

Role of Email in an Online Strategy

Brent Blackaby

In a new media era of web video, blogs, Facebook, and Twitter, there's a dark little secret: Email is still the workhorse, especially when it comes to online fundraising.

So as much as you spend time figuring out how to optimize your use of these new tools and reach new communities through these exciting new channels, don't neglect email as a core component of your online strategy.

Consider the most recent success in online politics: the Obama campaign. As much as the Obama campaign mastered the use of new media, taking advantage of the full range of online tools in their arsenal to engage supporters, the vast majority of the campaign's online contributions came in response to email solicitations.

Or consider another new media success story. On the Webb for Senate campaign in 2006, the campaign dynamic changed completely with the macaca video (www.youtube.com/watch?v=9G7gq7GQ71c). Blogs ran with it, mainstream media picked it up, and intense new attention was focused on a race that was now seen as winnable for Democrats.

At the same time, while blogs and press drove the overall narrative, it didn't directly impact the online fundraising operation. Roughly two-thirds of the campaign's online contributions came in response to email appeals.

That isn't to say that the blogs and media coverage didn't have a role – they certainly did. Increased coverage and attention led to an increase in sign-ups through the campaign website, which helped grow the base that we were marketing to through email. In addition, the coverage undoubtedly increased the likelihood that people already on the email list would respond with a contribution after receiving a solicitation, improving our conversion rate.

So press and blog coverage certainly helped tremendously – but email actually closed the deal when it came to fundraising.

Why is email still the "killer app" of online fundraising? With email, you're able to deliver a timely, relevant, impactful message directly to supporters' inboxes, with their permission, pushing them the content you want whenever you want.

Unlike Google, eBay, and Amazon.com, you can't rely on supporters being inspired enough to visit your website, learn about what's happening, and donate of their own volition. You have to meet them more than halfway, putting your content in their virtual hands in an environment where they're already spending time: their email inboxes.

But as important as email marketing is, it isn't easy. There are two central challenges for political campaigns when it comes to maximizing their email marketing efforts: (1) Building their email list, and (2) writing effective email appeals that inspire supporters to take action.

Building the Email List

Increasing the size of a campaign's email list, by identifying and drawing in as many supporters as you can, is probably the most important factor in increasing your online success.

After all, whether you're communicating with 5,000 people or 50,000 people the effort it takes to craft your message is the same – but the results can be dramatically different when going to a larger list.

The ultimate goal of your list-building effort should be to make it as easy as possible to sign-up – removing as many barriers as you can – while still "qualifying" potential supporters to make sure that the people who are signing up are really interested in your campaign.

That means, on the campaign website, make the sign-up process easy. Provide an email sign-up box right on the home page, where someone can submit their email address and maybe just their ZIP code, and then submit with one click. Or create a splash page before a visitor even gets to the main site to accomplish this.

Then pre-fill a longer sign-up form with the information from the fields the visitor has just submitted, so they're encouraged to provide more information, but you've still already captured their email address even if they decide not to complete the longer form. Even better, pre-fill a contribution or tell-a-friend form rather than just a longer sign-up form so you're "up-selling" a new supporter right away.

On that longer registration form, include as few fields there as you really need. Don't ask for 25 things – ask for a small handful, and make sure it's information you're really going to use. There's nothing that dissuades a website visitor more than a long, arduous form – even if a lot of the fields are "optional" and not required.

Next, I'm a big believer in the value of online advocacy campaigns – petitions, email-your-legislator asks, and the like. They serve a variety of important functions: to effectively brand a candidate in your supporters' minds based on these important advocacy issues, to engage your supporters in real action they can take to help your candidate on this issue (which deepens the relationship), and to provide a vehicle for targeted list-building (by encouraging people who share your candidate's view on an issue to participate and thereby join your email list).

So look for as many opportunities as you can to develop online advocacy campaigns – and then promote them far and wide. Email your existing list, encouraging supporters to participate and, as importantly, recruit their friends & family to participate. Share your advocacy campaigns with political blogs, by posting on blogs and running blog ads. Promote via search engine marketing, so that people searching for information on related keywords are prompted with an ad to your online advocacy campaign. And so on.

Another case study provides a good example. In July 2007, Senator Dick Durbin and Representative Rahm Emanuel teamed up to mobilize the public against British Petroleum's plans to increase its dumping of toxic chemicals into Lake Michigan. Senator Durbin and Rep. Emanuel waged a double-pronged online advocacy effort against the dumping plans, first launching an online letter writing campaign that targeted British Petroleum's CEO. Shortly thereafter, the Durbin team created a simple online petition, ProtectOurLake.com, to voice opposition to the plans.

After four weeks of aggressive online advocacy that generated more than 100,000 participants, supported by search engine ads and radio ads broadcast throughout the Chicago area that drove traffic to the online advocacy effort, British Petroleum reversed its plans. In the process, this online campaign generated nearly 65,000 new e-mail addresses for Senator Durbin's email list – people who shared his passion for this issue – and provided a tremendous opportunity to engage his pre-existing supporters.

Effective Email Appeals

In addition to growing your email list, the other important factor in a successful email program is crafting effective, well-written email appeals.

Consider email communications as a kind of marketing funnel, with steps that you're trying to optimize along the way.

The first thing you're trying to do is maximize the open rate – basically, to inspire as many supporters as you can to open the email in the first place.

Does your subject line stand out in a busy inbox? Is the sender someone who is trusted or recognized – or potentially stand out as someone new that the reader might want to hear from? Are you sending your email at a good time-of-day or day-of-week, which you may learn from testing over time? What has the recent frequency of email communications been – have you been bombarding folks, or is this the first time they've heard from you in a while? All of these things influence the open rate.

Next, once a supporter has opened your email, you're trying to maximize the click-through rate – the percentage of readers who click through to the action that you hope they'll take.

The click-through rate is impacted by the design of the email message itself. Is it visually appealing? Is the copy clear and compelling? Can a reader quickly scan the message and still take away key points? Do you have strong, frequent calls-to-action – and preferably calls-to-the-same-action – throughout? Is there a call-out box with a graphic or text that stands out to the reader's eye?

Lastly, once a supporter has actually clicked-through, the last thing you want to do is maximize the conversion rate at the end – get as many people as possible to complete the action page once they get there.

That means keeping the sign-up, contribution, or advocacy form as simple as possible, with as few fields as possible. It also means minimizing distractions and links to other pages from that action page, so a visitor's only choice is to complete that page, not to wander elsewhere. And make sure you've got a big "submit" button at the end that people want to click.

These are some of the basic questions to ask yourself as you're designing an effective email appeal for your campaign. Notice I said questions, not answers. That's because what works for one organization or campaign may not work for yours – and even what works for you may change over time as your list changes, as a campaign evolves, or as overall email communications expectations change.

But you're in luck: Email is one of the most easily-tracked marketing vehicles around. So you should test and re-test as much as possible – with every email you send if you can – to figure out what's working, and incorporate those learnings into subsequent email communications.

Summary

There's no doubt about it: After the success of the Obama campaign in 2008, all political campaigns are now expected to have a presence in many different online communications channels: Facebook, YouTube, Twitter, the blogosphere, search engines, and many others.

But as much as you're building a robust new media operation that takes advantage of all of these new online tools, make sure you don't neglect the old workhorse that's still powering every successful online political campaign:

Your email program!

Social Networks Eclipse E-Mail

By Teddy Wayne

The New York Times

May 18, 2009 page B3

Alongside the explosive growth of online video over the last six years, time spent on social networks surpassed that for e-mail for the first time in February, signaling a paradigm shift in consumer engagement with the Internet.

According to a report released in April by Nielsen, Internet use for "short-tail" sites with large audience reach has evolved since 2003. The change is from portal-oriented sites, like shopping directories and Internet tools like Microsoft Passport, to social networks, YouTube and providers of niche content.

In November 2007, the video audience also exceeded the e-mail audience for the first time, and sites with long-form videos (averaging six to eight minutes) are showing much more growth and user time spent online than those with shorter videos…

Although Charles Buchwalter, senior vice president for research and analytics for Nielsen, said marketers had yet to master advertising on social media, he predicted that "over the next 12 months a model will emerge" that takes into account "the influence factor" of users who wield disproportionate power.

CHAPTER 24

Lead Generation
Identifies Voters

Tony Winders

Lead Generation Overview

In political consulting, it is perhaps best known as "building the base," "constituent building" or simply "database marketing."In the world of online advertising, "lead generation" represents approximately $1.6 billion of the $23 billion online advertising marketplace.

Online lead generation is the practice of generating qualified leads for advertisers by introducing their information to consumers while they are in the process of registering their information for other purposes, such as purchasing a product, signing up for an e-mail list or entering an online promotion. Upon completing the registration process, they are presented with advertisers' offers and invited to choose whether they would like to receive additional information from that advertiser. The form data collected, or some portion thereof, is then delivered to the advertiser in a secure environment on a cost-per-lead basis.

While the online advertising trade refers to the category as "lead generation," the term can be confusing because it also refers to a primary campaign objective for most marketers. For this reason, it is important to note the distinction between building databases of consumers who opt in to receive information from advertisers while they are registering on other sites, from registering users directly on an advertiser's web site, regardless of how they got there. This chapter deals solely with the former.

Lead Generation in Political Marketing Online

In the political arena, online lead generation has been used most successfully by advocacy groups and nonprofit organizations to identify individuals sympathetic to a particular cause. Although it can be used to build e-mail lists or offline marketing databases of voters, historically political candidates have not utilized the lead generation channel. This is likely due to the fact that candidates have other proven ways to obtain lists of likely supporters, or because the channel is once removed from more commonly used online tactics such as search engine marketing and display advertising.

In cases where it is more difficult to identify individuals sympathetic to a particular cause, the lead generation channel has proven to be an effective way for online consumers to choose whether or not they wish to receive more information.

The primary ways lead generation can help political organizations include:

- Building e-mail and offline subscriber databases
- Driving letter writing campaigns
- Conducting surveys for research purposes
- Creating awareness of an issue, party or candidate
- Identifying and organizing volunteers

While lead generation is a highly effective way to identify consumers who are interested in a particular issue, ultimately it is the responsibility of the political marketing organization to fully capitalize on the leads that are generated. Lead generation is recommended for marketers who have a method in place to follow up on leads by phone, e-mail or direct mail.

Similarly, while lead generation can build awareness of a candidate's key issues and build large databases of people sympathetic to their ideology, is not ideal for fundraising, since ultimately consumers must be won over by a candidate's message and the request for a donation is more successful among constituents who are already enrolled in their agenda.

How Lead Generation Works

Consumers, or in political terms, constituents or voters, are introduced to a marketer's message by online publishers who agree to promote an offer or advertisement within their sites. Publishers are paid on a cost-per-lead basis, and advertisers only pay when qualified leads are delivered.

The advertising creative itself can be displayed in the form of banner ads, direct e-mail correspondence or search engine marketing listings, which lead a consumer directly to a registration page on the advertiser's site, or a page hosted by a lead generation vendor that appears to be integrated with the site.

Another popular method is to place ads, also known in online advertising jargon as "offers" in a co-registration path. Co-registration is the method of displaying offers to consumers immediately after they have completed a registration such as a purchase or entry into a promotion, and the lead is subsequently transferred to the advertisers with whom the consumer has agreed to receive additional information.

In all cases, the desired objective is to obtain a consumer's contact information and permission to follow up with them about a particular offer, candidate, cause or company.

In order to drive scale through this channel, marketers contract with lead generation vendors, or networks, who have agreements with many sites or publishers. These vendors play an important role in aggregating audiences, monitoring lead quality, securely delivering leads and the all of the associated campaign management, delivery, reporting and accounting functions.

What kind of data is collected?

Lead generation data typically includes basic contact information such as:

- Name
- Street address
- City
- State
- ZIP
- E-mail addresses
- Birth date
- Gender

For an additional fee, custom questions can be asked to further qualify consumers' interest in and eligibility for a particular offer. In the political arena, such questions may include party affiliation and political views, occupation, income level.

Anything a political marketer would want to know about its constituents can likely be asked, but the more qualified an audience becomes, the smaller it gets. This is an issue of quality versus scale that every lead generation marketer must contend with, and that political direct marketers know best from years of offline experience. Through the process of testing, and with the advice of sophisticated lead generation vendors who use technology and experience what is most likely to perform, marketers can quickly determine the performance metrics necessary to drive a scalable lead generation campaign.

Lead Nurturing

Lead generation, especially when part of an efficient database marketing operation can be a highly effective and scalable tool for communicating ideas and building lists around particular causes or issues. But collecting data is just the beginning of the process. To fully leverage the investment in this powerful online marketing tactic it is critical for there to be an effective means of following up with leads, no matter what the size of the organization or budget. Whether to follow up by phone, e-mail or postal mail is a matter of strategy best determined by each advertiser. Because each player in the value chain is motivated to make campaigns perform, some lead generation providers offer creative resources and tools to assist with how messages are responded to online in the days following the initial acquisition of a lead.

Targeting Options

The primary targeting options available for lead generation campaigns are demographic and geographic, however the offers most likely to achieve scale into the hundreds of thousands (or millions) of leads are those which have resonance with a national consumer audience. The more targeting parameters are applied, the higher the cost per lead and the fewer leads will be delivered. For political marketers, however, audiences in the thousands (or hundreds) can hold enormous value, making the lower volume and higher priced leads extremely worthwhile.

While some providers can target banner and other advertising creative prior to a consumer having completed a registration form through the use of IP-based targeting technology, the most common practice is to serve offers in a particular area based on ZIP code information provided by the consumer as part of the registration process. Similarly, demographic targeting can be used to present offers only to those individuals who have identified themselves as being of a particular age or gender.

Data Filtering and Validation

The top lead generation vendors have multiple processes in place for removing unqualified leads and confirming leads delivered to advertisers are of the highest quality possible.

The best practices of basic lead validation include:

- Removing duplicate leads
- E-mail domain name verification
- Verifying city, state, ZIP code combinations
- Verifying phone numbers by matching states with area
  codes.

More advanced forms of lead validation include checking leads again the U.S. Postal Service database and contracting with third party data vendors with access to more consumer data from which to match the name of an individual with the contact information they provided.

Compliance and Data Security

Because lead generation data includes personally identifiable information, how it is collected and shared is subject to the scrutiny of consumer privacy advocacy groups and federal regulators and legislators. Before starting a lead generation campaign, political organizations should draft a privacy policy and terms and conditions that contain valid contact information and are consistent with industry standards, easily accessible for review by consumers and fully transparent with respect to the collection, use and sharing of consumer information. In addition, it should clearly state how to complete the advertiser's offer, how to opt out of data collection, use and sharing, and should provide clear definitions with respect to how data will be shared with third parties.

Interactive Advertising Bureau

Through the efforts of its Lead Generation Committee, the Interactive Advertising Bureau has taken an active role in helping to define guidelines and best practices for the online lead generation marketing industry. Its most recent papers "IAB Online Lead Generation: Lead Quality Accountability Best Practices for Advertisers and Publishers" and "B2C and B2B Best Practices for U.S.-based Advertisers and Publishers" provide a more detailed examination of the lead generation industry and can be found on the IAB web site at www.iab.net.

Lead Generation Vendors

There have been references to lead generation providers throughout this chapter. Among the most notable lead generation vendors today are:

ValueClickMedia - valueclickmedia.com/adv_lead_generation.shtml
Webclients - www.webclients.net
Active Response Group - www.activeresponsegroup.com
Q Interactive - www.qinteractive.com
The Useful - theuseful.com
Permission Data - www.permissiondata.com
CoregMedia - coregmedia.com
Connexus - www.connexuscorp.com

Conclusion

Among the wide range of tactics available to political marketers, lead generation is just one of many online advertising options. For organizations with a mass consumer appeal and the resources to properly manage and nurture contacts generated through this channel, lead generation can be a highly effective means of increasing awareness and quickly growing scalable databases of consumers who have asked to receive more information about a particular issue, cause or candidate.

Lead Generation Case Study

Client: Blind

Agency: **MSHC Partners**

Lead Generation Vendor: **ValueClick Media**

Objective: **Petition Signatures**

For a member-based association whose objective was to influence an upcoming state senate vote, MHSC Partners developed a lead generation solution to obtain signatures for a petition among constituents in affected by the pending healthcare legislation.

With a campaign goal to obtain legally verifiable petition signatures, lead generation was an obvious fit for its ability to obtain registration data from consumers. Targeting criteria established for the campaign included geo-targeting to the state level, and contact information requested included first name, last name, e-mail address and ZIP code. No additional targeting was applied and no additional fields of data were requested.

Simple text ads and static graphic images were presented to consumers, inviting them to sign the petition and promote the vote's goals. During the three-week campaign, the target 7,500 signatures were acquired. According to MHSC interactive media buyer Jenny Myers, "We reached our goal to have the petition signatures viewed by all of the relevant state lawmakers and we're confident it is having a meaningful impact on the legislative process."

CHAPTER 25

Best Practices
of Search

Ben Weisberg

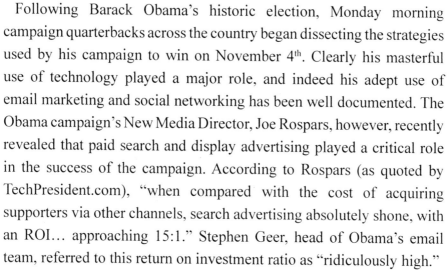

Following Barack Obama's historic election, Monday morning campaign quarterbacks across the country began dissecting the strategies used by his campaign to win on November 4th. Clearly his masterful use of technology played a major role, and indeed his adept use of email marketing and social networking has been well documented. The Obama campaign's New Media Director, Joe Rospars, however, recently revealed that paid search and display advertising played a critical role in the success of the campaign. According to Rospars (as quoted by TechPresident.com), "when compared with the cost of acquiring supporters via other channels, search advertising absolutely shone, with an ROI… approaching 15:1." Stephen Geer, head of Obama's email team, referred to this return on investment ratio as "ridiculously high."

Obama's success was not unique: the McCain campaign publicly reported returns of three or four dollars for every dollar spent online; Jeanne Shaheen in New Hampshire reported 7:1 returns; and Senator Mitch McConnell's reelection campaign in Kentucky yielded astonishing 30:1 returns on search advertising, according to the ad agencies that ran their online advertising campaigns.

When voters are looking for information about a candidate or issue, or seek an opportunity to engage, donate or support a political cause, their search often begins online. Capturing this opportunity necessitates an understanding of the basics of search advertising. Though no search engine will promise Obama-like results for everyone, there are best practices concerning proper creative and keyword list creation for the elections and issue advocacy community.

Before we dive in, however, let's define some of our terms. What do we mean when we say "paid search advertising?" The broadest definition of the term refers to the placement of ads next to the results of an online search. These ads generally appear to the right or above the organic (unpaid) results on search engines such as Google or Yahoo. Typically, these ads are small, with two or three lines of text and a URL, and are "pay-per-click" (PPC), which means that the advertiser pays only when a searcher clicks on an ad and goes to the advertiser's webpage. If your ad appears and no one clicks on it, you receive the ad impression for free.

Do not worry about "over-bidding" as all of the major search engines use what are called "Dutch auctions," wherein all clicks are automatically discounted to just one cent higher than the next highest bid. Because PPC advertising is an auction model, bidding high will help determine your position on the results page. The more you are willing to pay, the higher up in the paid search listings you will appear.

However, with Google's paid search program your bid is only half the battle: the second key factor that determines your ad's position is the oft-misunderstood Quality Score (QS). Google, like the other major search engines, strives to show as relevant an ad as possible - "the right ad, to the right person, at the right time," as Google CEO Eric Schmidt often says. This will create a virtuous cycle that is good for the user, good for the advertiser, and good for Google. Though the formula is complex, a high click through rate (the number of times an ad is clicked on divided by the number of searches in which it appears) is a major factor in quality score. Therefore, ads with high click through rates are rewarded with lower CPCs and better placement on the page.

So, how much does a search campaign cost? The good news is that because it is a pay-per-click model the answer is largely up to you. Cap your investment at $10 per day and your ad will stop appearing after $10 worth of clicks; spend $100 a day and you may reach ten times the number of people and drive ten times the traffic to your site.

Getting started with an AdWords campaign is as easy as going to Adwords.Google.com and clicking "Start now." Choose a login email and password and enter a credit card number and you are ready to go— the process is similar with YSM and Microsoft Ad Center. The first, and most important step, in building your campaign will be to choose your keywords. Keywords are the terms you choose that tell the system when to serve your ad. Would you like your ad to appear when a user types "campaign finance" into the search box? "Get out the vote"? Having a strong keyword list is the most crucial aspect of ensuring your ad gets put in front of the right audience and is frequently a pain point for beginning search marketers.

The most common mistake is having an overly broad keyword list. For example, a senate campaign using keywords like "election," "politics," or "taxes." Instead, start with a narrower keyword list that is specific to your campaign. For example: "john doe for senate" or "new york senate race." Narrower terms like these will be more relevant and will likely lead to a higher click through rate and quality score.

Not everyone is looking for such specific terms so after establishing a solid foundation of good quality terms, you may want to add additional keywords. The key is to expand reach while maintaining relevancy. Doing this successfully depends on your marketing goals and budget: are you looking to attract a wide audience? Do you have the budget to have a meaningful presence on broader, more competitive keywords?

If you are looking to expand—many advanced campaigns will have tens of thousands of keywords—there are several directions in which to go. Misspellings, plurals, and synonyms are usually a good place to start ("jonathan doe for senate"), and frequently have quality scores similar to their properly spelled, singular cousins.

Next, try using a keyword tool, like one that Google offers, to help grow your list. Simply enter a keyword or two, and the tool will return a generous list of related terms that users tend to search on after searching for your original term.

Your keyword list now complete (or at least a work in progress – breaking news, campaign events, and new campaign messages and ads are all reasons to update your list continually), it is time to develop your paid search ad. Successful paid search ads are deceptively simple: the most common error is trying to write eye-catching, overblown, ad text.

A paid search ad with less than 100 characters is not suited to such an approach, and too often people resort to gimmicky punctuation or unusual syntax. You have already attracted the right user because you have chosen relevant keywords, now you simply need to show the user that you do, in fact, have the most relevant content to their query. For example, someone who searches "jon doe for senate" or "new york senate race" has already qualified themselves as a target for your message. Now you must guide them, rather than strong-arm them, to your site.

Again, keep it simple:

Jon Doe for New York

Get the Facts on the Issues That

Matter to You. Learn More Today.

JonDoeforSenate.com

While simplicity is key, there are other best practices for good quality ad text. Capitalize key terms in your advertising creative and

URL, and use a strong call to action by telling the user exactly what you would like them to do: "Sign our Petition Today," "Learn More on our Site," "Donate Now," etc. Find keywords that you believe will be most frequently searched and put them in your ad text. This will draw the advertiser's eye to your ad, and, as if to emphasize the point, most search engines will automatically bold that word. Use details in your ad text that are unique to your campaign or group: are you the oldest, newest or largest organization of your type? It will lend credibility to your ad if you say so.

Do not waste precious real estate by putting your URL in the body of the ad; there is a line for that at the end. Use a destination URL that is most relevant to the keywords in your campaign. If your ad specifically references the economy, direct users to the page on your site where you discuss the economy.

Finally, test your creative: most programs allow you to automatically rotate several ad units at once, giving you the ability to test audience response to different slogans and wording. Within a short period of time you will discover which version performs best.

To summarize, with keywords, ad text and landing pages keep it specific, and keep it tightly themed. Have one campaign with keywords and ad text about one specific topic (carbon emissions, say), and link your ads to the page on your site that specifically discusses that theme; do the same for the next theme (solar power, clean coal technology, etc.), and repeat until you have covered all of your key issues.

The 2008 presidential election has forced all future political and public affairs campaigns to rethink how they use technology to reach and motivate supporters. Facebook profiles, YouTube video uploads, and tweets on Twitter are now necessary components of the political toolbox – search advertising, too, has become an essential part of the new 21st Century campaign. Eric Frenchman, Chief Internet

Strategist at Connell Donatelli and a consultant for the McCain for President campaign, recently told National Journal, "I cannot think of a reason why anybody who is running for an elected office or involved in issue marketing would not spend significant money in search advertising."[1] We couldn't agree more.

CHAPTER 26

When Search Engine Marketing Matters in Politics

Corina Constantin, Ph.D.
Kevin Lee

The prominent use of the Internet in the 2008 US presidential election signaled a substantial shift in the form and structure of political campaigning and civic engagement. Not since the iconic Kennedy-Nixon televised debates of 1960 have we seen such an overhaul in the *modus operandi* of presidential candidates. For the first time in the history of US presidential elections, candidates have made the Internet the primary means of disseminating information to the general public, organizing and communicating with their supporters, enabling networking among supporters, and fundraising.

The impact of the Internet throughout the 2008 campaigns has been quite unprecedented. The online medium has transformed political communication and facilitated political engagement as never before, by shifting the focus from a TV-like one-to-many model of presenting information about candidates to an extraordinary combination of one-to-one, one-to-many, many-to-one, and many-to-many channels. Among them, much of the influence can be attributed to search engines, as one of the first online touch points. With many media consumers turning to online sources for political information, comScore estimated, for example, that "Obama" was used as a search term more than 5.36 million times on average per month between January and June 2008, while "McCain" was used more than 1.34 million times per month during the same period (www.comscore.com). What differentiated the 2008 election from earlier ones, however, was not as much the public's appetite for the Internet (e.g., the average search index for "Kerry" and "Bush" was similar to the one for "Obama" and "McCain," according to Google Trends), but rather the interest of the candidates themselves to adopt it and to heavily promote themselves online. As an example, the use of sponsored links to advertise candidates and positions has seen a dramatic increase in 2008 compared to 2004.

While it was reasonable to expect political candidates to follow their audiences where they were (namely, online), this significant increase in Internet usage for campaigning purposes begs the question of how effective the online medium is in political communication and *how much does the Web overall, and search engines in particular, influence attitudes, preferences, and behaviors when it comes to voting choices.*

Didit Labs put that to test for a few days during the Democratic and Republican National Conventions, when we conducted a study meant to connect online search behaviors with the attitudes and voting preferences of Internet users. During this time (August 26th – 28th and September 3rd, 2008), we set up search marketing campaignsin the three top-tier engines, with ad group themes centered around candidate names, the presidential election, and election polls. The landing page consisted of an online survey that asked questions related to respondents' online search behaviors directed toward obtaining political information, their attitudes and preferences concerning search engines and other online sources, and their political attitudes and voting preferences.

The interest of the public in this election was obvious; during the approximately 42 hours during which the search campaigns were running, we gathered 877,320 impressions and 17,797 clicks through Google (2.03% CTR), 216,150 impressions and 2,990 clicks through Yahoo (1.38% CTR), and 87,063 impressions and 1,206 clicks through MSN Live (1.39% CTR). Moreover, the US elections have sparked a wide interest outside US as well, with a few clicks coming from countries such as Canada, Japan, Israel, UK, Germany and France, among others (for a complete list, see Table1). All questionnaires completed by searchers ineligible to vote in the US (non-US citizens, younger than 18) have been subsequently discarded and were not included in any of the reports.

Country	Visits	Country (contd.)	Visits
Argentina	2		
Australia	3	Kenya	4
Austria	1	Korea, Republic of	2
Bahamas	3	Kuwait	1
Barbados	1	Lebanon	1
Belgium	2	Libyan Arab Jamahiriya	2
Bosnia and Herzegovina	1	Malaysia	1
Brazil	1	Namibia	1
Canada	201	Netherlands	4
China	2	Netherlands Antilles	1
Colombia	3	Nigeria	2
Costa Rica	1	Norway	1
Denmark	1	Panama	2
Dominican Republic	1	Philippines	4
Ethiopia	2	Poland	1
France	10	Puerto Rico	4
Germany	14	Satellite Provider	11
Ghana	1	Serbia	1
Greece	1	Sierra Leone	1
Guam	1	Spain	1
Guyana	2	Sweden	1
Haiti	4	Thailand	1
Iceland	2	Trinidad and Tobago	1
Indonesia	1	United Arab Emirates	2
Ireland	5	United Kingdom	20
Israel	35	United States	23152
Italy	1	Venezuela	1
Japan	101	Virgin Islands, U.S.	1

The survey was displayed on four different pages, with 4,151 respondents completing the first page (18.87% response rate), and 3,075 respondents completing all four pages of the questionnaire (25.92% survey mortality or drop-out rate). While the sample was a convenience sample (e.g., it consisted entirely of volunteers that were highly interested in the topic and more likely to be politically involved than the general public) and thus posed the problem of self-selection bias, it offered great insight into the attitudes and preferences of heavy consumers of online political information. The high political engagement of the respondents was clearly shown in the composition of the sample: 96.78% of the participants were registered to vote and likely to vote. The sample also contained a relatively larger number of independents than expected (obviously in search of more information about the candidates) with a fair number of Democrats and Republicans, and a slightly larger number of female than male respondents.

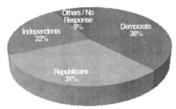

Figure 1: Self-reported political affiliation of survey respondents

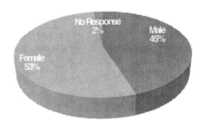

Figure 2: Gender frequency of survey respondents

When asked what their primary source of political information was, the majority of respondents indicated cable TV (57.94%), while others the Internet (19.08%) or broadcast TV (17.90%). Overall, cable TV as one of the top three sources of political information for 84.34% of respondents, the Internet for 79.19%, broadcast TV for 66.78% and newspapers for 54.13% of all respondents (for more information, see figure 3). Among the online sources, news sites were the most prominent source of information, with 67.57% of respondents declaring that they visit them often, followed by search engines (visited by 43.51% of respondents) and candidate websites (visited by 29.39% of respondents; see figure 4)

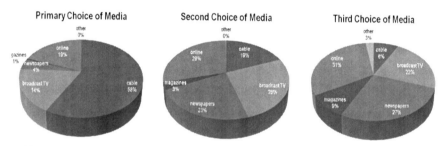

Figure 3: Top three media chosen as sources of political information

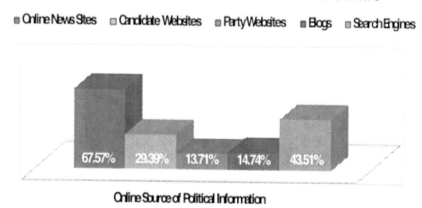

Figure 4: Top online sources of political information

As with other types of searches, respondents preferred Google to other engines when looking for political information, rating Google the highest in both frequency of use and relevance, followed by Yahoo, MSN Live, AOL, and Ask.

Table 2: Means and standard deviations for frequency of use and relevance ratings of various search engines

	Google	Yahoo	MSN	Ask	AOL
Usage	6.45	3.79	2.69	1.36	2.09
	-3.85	-3.79	-3.32	-2.01	-2.97
	$F_{Greenhouse-Geisser}$ (3.568, 18307.977) = 1896.383, p < .001, partial η^2=.314				
Relevance	6.61	4.91	3.56	2.53	2.86
	-3.5	-3.71	-3.44	-2.87	-3.14
	$F_{Greenhouse-Geisser}$ (3.534, 9751.914) = 1290.207, p < .001, partial η^2=.296				

Not surprisingly after a long primaries season, very few people were still uncertain and reported to be somewhat likely or very likely to change their voting preferences between the time of the survey and November 4th. Thus, only 2.85% of respondents declared that they might and 3.29% of them thought it very likely to change their opinions, whereas the overwhelming majority (83.89%) thought it very unlikely to shift voting preferences to a different candidate (see figure 5). Although a very small minority (6.14%), those whose attitudes are subject to change are oftentimes able to radically influence election results, and are or should be vigorously targeted by political candidates.

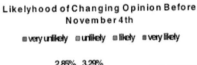

Likelyhood of Changing Opinion Before November 4th

■ very unlikely ■ unlikely ■ likely ■ very likely

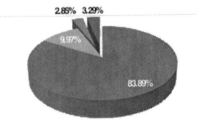

Figure 5: Self-declared likelihood of opinion change

The question then becomes how to effectively reach these potentially undecided voters when they are online. While chances for their shifting of voting preferences to a different candidate are relatively slim, selecting links that favor the opposing party seems the most effective way of changing opinions, while selecting links that support the preferred candidate decreases that likelihood. In our survey, selecting links favoring the opposition increased the likelihood of changing ones' political opinions by 29.58%, while selecting links supporting a favorite candidate decreased it by 14.80% for all respondents. When only respondents that mentioned the Internet as one of their top three media choices for obtaining political information were included, selecting links favoring the opposition increased the likelihood of changing ones' political opinions by 38.78%, while selecting links supporting a favorite candidate decreased it by 15.46%.

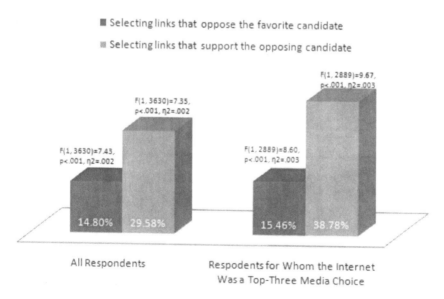

Figure 6: Likelihood of changing one's political opinion given the types of links selected

Within this context, it seems all the more relevant that most respondents start their online search for political information with the search engines and news sites, and that search engines become more predominant in the search endeavors of those who place the Internet as one of their top three media choices and even more predominant for those who place the Internet as their top choice.

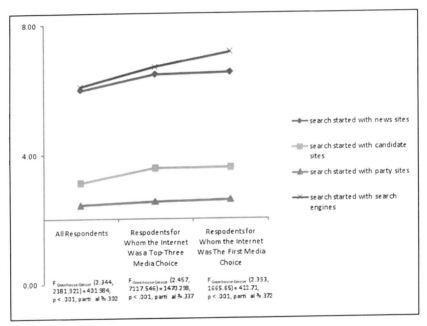

Figure 7: Preference in first online touch points based on media choices

The task of the political communicator becomes seemingly more difficult in persuading the independent voters, as they tend to be more suspicious of sponsored links than others. When asked when they thought of sponsored links, self-reported independent voters rated sponsored links less favorably than other participants did on several dimensions.

For example, they considered sponsored links to be less useful, less relevant, less helpful, and less informative than both Democrats and Republicans. However, these self-reports have to be taken with a good dose of caution, as approximately half of the self-indentified Independents have also affirmed that they never click on sponsored links, although, incidentally, they had just clicked one in order to arrive at the survey page. As an ironic side note, 47.20% of all respondents stated that they had never clicked on a sponsored link before, 12.50% did not know what sponsored links were, and only 25.30% admitted to having used sponsored links at least once – all this while the survey could only have been reached via sponsored links.

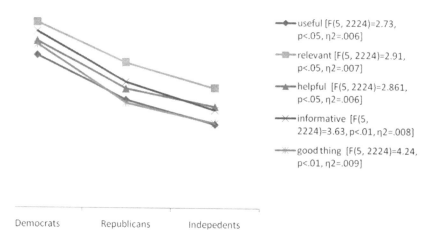

useful [F(5, 2224)=2.73, p<.05, η2=.006]

relevant [F(5, 2224)=2.91, p<.05, η2=.007]

helpful [F(5, 2224)=2.861, p<.05, η2=.006]

informative [F(5, 2224)=3.63, p<.01, η2=.008]

good thing [F(5, 2224)=4.24, p<.01, η2=.009]

Democrats   Republicans   Indepedents

Figure 8: Perceptions of sponsored links among respondents of different political affiliations

This raises the question of whether search engine users are aware of the nature of the link clicked, especially when it is displayed on the side of the results page rather than on top of the natural/organic links. While a puzzling finding, this failure to identify sponsored links by a significant number of searchers may have contributed to their success in the electoral campaign, since mistaking persuasive attempts for other link types could also mean a lower resistance to their influence.

All these findings indicate that while many people might not be likely to admit to being subject to persuasion, their extensive use of the Internet in looking for political information makes the online medium a natural choice for political advertising. Within a wide array of online political forms of promotion, sponsored links in particular should occupy a central role not only because search engines are the predominant first online touch points, but also because of the apparent willingness of political searchers to pursue them. Of course, not only the form, but also the content of political advertising matters considerably: content praising a political candidate other than one's current choice is more likely to change one's voting preferences than, let's say, denigrating one's favorite.

Use of Sponsored Links

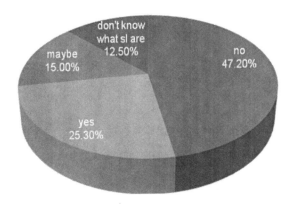

Figure 9: Used of sponsored links (at least once)

CHAPTER 27

Media Fragmentation: What it Means for Political Campaigns

Jason R. Krebs

So let's state the obvious: The media world has become fragmented. Ok, that sounds like a fairly harmless statement that's spoken by media big shots and financial analysts. But what does it really mean? And after we decide what it means, does it really matter? And if it matters, what will be the ramifications for companies and consumers?

So let's begin with the recent casual history of media and communication: books, newspapers, magazines, radio, movies, telephone, television, cb radio (c.b. stands for citizens' band, how many of you knew that?), on line services, PDA's, ipods, and finally the Internet.

Here are the respective dates of when our media platforms came upon the landscape. Usually I am not one who is only interested in domestic affairs, and I have never been interested in revisionist history, but for the purposes of fluidity, fact checking and relevance to what we're looking to accomplish here, let's keep our focus on US only. Another caveat one has to deal with, as history is known to present, while of course there can only be one "first" of anything; there are many people who often claim such a position.

So the below represents a fair, unbiased interpretation of what appears to be the most salient historical data:

- The First newspaper was the Boston News-Letter, which published its first issue on April 24, 1704
- The first magazine went on sale in Philadelphia on Feb 13, 1741 — aptly named "The American Magazine."
- The first telephone in 1871 patented by Meucci (we know that all Italians hate having their heritage robbed of this important historical detail). On Oct 9, 1876 Alexander Bell made the first call to a receiver over 2 miles away.
- The first commercially successful, movie projector in the U.S. appeared in 1896, called the Vitascope projector.
- The first radio news program was broadcast August 31, 1920 by station 8MK in Detroit, Michigan.
- The first regularly scheduled television service in the United States began on July 2, 1928.
- The CB radio came into view in the US in the 1960's.
- Online services, AOL, Compuserve and Prodigy arrived in the early to mid 1980's.
- The commercial Internet's World Wide Web launched in 1991.
- The PDA (Personal Digital Assistant) first came on the landscape in 1983, and believed to be first referred to as such in 1992 regarding the Apple Newton.
- The iPod was launched on October 23, 2001.

OK, now all of the relevant platforms are identified, it would make sense to take a look at how people are using such devices.

Time Spent Online per Week by US At-Home Internet Users, 2000-2007 (average hours)

Year	Hours
2000	3.3
2001	5.9
2002	6.8
2003	6.9
2005	7.8
2006	8.9
2007	15.3

Note: *usage for any reason, including but not limited to non-work-related
Source: USC Annenberg School Center for the Digital Future, "The 2008
Digital Future Project-Year Seven" as cited in press release, February 18,
2008

092478   www.eMarketer.com

As you would expect, the frequency with which people are now accessing the Internet from ones own home has increased dramatically. It's not enough to see that this has happened. We must look at why this has happened, as well as how. The primary reason for this is the increased ability of broadband access in people's homes. This has opened up a dramatic gateway for personal usage of the Internets unlimited supply of nooks and crannies. In the recent past, employers were believed to be shouldering the bandwidth load for these sometimes notorious time wasters.

Some of you may recall an early product called PointCast that took over your monitor as a screen saver. It was wonderfully designed and totally customizable for sports, weather, news, stocks, etc. the problem with this product though was that it was a "bandwidth hog" and internal I.T. departments hated it for that very reason; it made their whole network slow down. Many companies then denied their employees access altogether.

My point in mentioning this not only points out a good product before it's time, but also the levels of acceptability in the workplace of leisure reading vs. business reading. Years ago would it have been frowned upon to be at one's desk reading the day's newspaper? What about a trade magazine? I am old enough to remember that practice being well accepted in the workplace, but now I can assuredly point out that walking through an office now and seeing someone with a newspaper sprayed across their desk would get a fair share of awkward glances. However, someone can now read digital communications for hours and hours without being caught by onlookers. I believe the phrase NSFW –NotSafe For Work-- was invented as a result of the Internet.

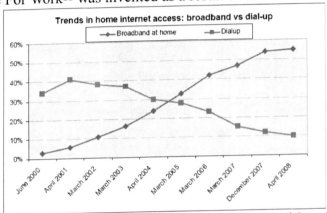

Now that the usage has also moved to people's homes, it's only natural that something else has to be given up as the hours in the week continue to remain stubbornly constant. I am hardly an anthropologist, so I'll leave the larger social implications to others, but here are the facts of yearly, hourly usage of the most frequented media.

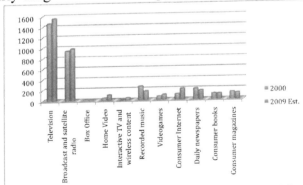

Television still continues to dominate the landscape. More channels, diverse programming and better technology have helped to maintain its dominant position in the media landscape. Whatever potential decreases in usage the industry watchdogs may have been predicting from the advent of Tivo and DVR's (digital video recorders), has actually not materialized. In my own editorial and market survey of one, I will tell you that my usage of TV has actually increased as a result of my DVR. Watching shows at the times that I choose to watch them has dramatically increased my enjoyment of the medium. Watching the commercials on the other hand, is a story for another chapter. Not to be outdone in the importance of televisions continued grip on the landscape is also without a doubt the advent of HD (high definition) programming as well as new and affordable flat screen and/or plasma TV's. A buzzword in the industry is to determine at which screen someone is looking (tv, computer or mobile phone). At some point in the future though the merging of the computer screen and the tv is inevitable. 50 years from now will people even call it TV?

The drop in the music businesses market share is the story of the ages. The technology industry has played both friend and foe to the music world with the overall future of the industry still puzzling to the average consumer. On the one hand, more people may listen to music now than ever before thanks to the ipod. But $.99 songs have forever replaced the purchase of the $15.99 album.

The ramifications of this are huge to those in the business. In the past, when someone heard a good song and was compelled to purchase the album to get it, all of the waste was still paid for. Now, no waste. Or as a music executive would tell you, no profit. The music industry now sees it's future less in the profit of recorded music paid for by consumers and more in the margins of licensing, live tours and sponsorships.

The so called "old media" of books, magazines and newspapers have seen the most evident decline of consumption over the past decade with many experts continuing to predict that pattern to continue. But without those collective industries providing the content that's consumed in the internet/digital space, we absolutely would not have seen the explosion in Internet usage over the same time frame.

Cell phone	73%
Desktop computer	68
Digital camera	55
Video camera	43
Laptop computer	30
iPod or other MP3 player	20
Webcam	13
Blackberry, Palm, or other personal digital assistant	11

Now the "what" comes into play. A major question exists in asking what people are doing now that this Internet thing is here. Are we doing old things differently or are we doing new things in new ways? If someone merely switched watching 5 hours per week of nightly network news on TV, to the same programs that are now available on the internet, it might not be as dramatic a shift. In that scenario, all it takes are some savvy business leaders to shift their attention to where their consumers are. But when that same person turns 5 hours of TV news time into time spent reading independent blogs, checking email, or uploading his/her own video, well then you have a real consumption shift that will have domino effects up and down the line.

So let's take a look at what people are doing in their respective personal time with digital media.

Online Activities:
Share of users in each category who do listed activity on the typical day

	All internet users	Dial-up at home	Broadband at home (all respondents)	Access Internet away from home or work using WiFi on laptop computer
Use an online search engine	49%	26%	57%	68%
Check weather reports and forecasts	30	14	36	44
Get news online	39	18	47	54
Visit a state or local government website	13	4	16	20
Look online for information about the 2008 election	23	10	27	33
Watch a video on a video-sharing site like YouTube or GoogleVideo	16	5	20	28
Look online for information about a job	6	4	6	10
Send instant messages	13	6	16	23
Read someone else's blog	11	3	15	17
Use a social networking site like MySpace, Facebook, or LinkedIn.com	13	7	16	20
Make a donation to charity online	1	0	2	2
Downloaded a podcast	3	1	4	6
Download or share files using peer-to-peer networks such as BiTorrent or LiveWire	3	2	3	4
Create or work on your own blog	5	3	6	9
Number of cases	1553	249	1138	504

Source: Pew Internet & American Life Project Survey, April 2008.

At this point, it's important to look at the major sources of revenue for this group. Advertising isn't the only piece of the equation that funds the media world, though it's a large source. Newspapers and magazines certainly have subscriptions, but rarely do these cover anything more than the costs of printing and delivery. Cable companies are much more lucrative with subscription fees and now delivering high-speed Internet and phone service. The web model however, is almost universally an advertising supported business.

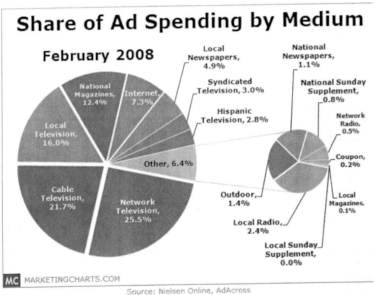

- Internet spending estimates are from AdRelevance; all others from Nielsen Monitor-Plus. Different methodologies employed by each company may lead to disproportionate comparisons.

Ad Spending by Medium - Medium Share of Spending

Network Television	25.5%
Cable Television	21.7%
Local Television	16.0%
National Magazines	12.4%
Internet	7.3%
Local Newspapers	4.9%
Syndicated Television	3.0%
Hispanic Television	2.8%
Local Radio	2.4%
Outdoor	1.4%
National Newspapers	1.1%
National Sunday Supplement	0.8%
Network Radio	0.5%
Coupon	0.2%
Local Magazines	0.1%
Local Sunday Supplement	0.0%

To show you one of the more dramatic examples of revenue flight of traditional media to the Internet here is the most telling statistics:

Newspaper Classified Ad Revenue (1980-2008)	
Year	Revenue in Million $
1980	$4222
1985	8375
1990	11500
1995	13742
2000	19608
2005	17312
2008	9975
Source: NAA Business Analysis & Research, May 2009	

In the business executive parlance, that's what's known as "falling off a cliff." The loss of classifieds revenue to newspapers has caused a dramatic shift in their fortunes. Newspaper executives were largely unprepared to deal with this seismic shift in their business models which will never recover. What's more telling in this example is that the revenue was not lost to another entity using the same model online, but one that was completely different as "Craig's List" appeared as a free product, turning billions in newspaper profit (70-85% margin) into dust.

News No Longer Newspaper's Forte

According to the Pew Research Center for the People & the Press, the Internet has now surpassed all other media except television as an outlet for national and international news. Currently, 40% of the survey respondents say they get most of their news about national and international issues from the internet, up from just 24% in September 2007. For the first time in a Pew survey, more people say they rely mostly on the internet for news than cite newspapers. Television continues to be cited most frequently as a main source for national and international news.

National and International New Sources (% of Respondents)			
Year	Television	Newspaper	Internet
2001	74%	45%	13%
2002	82	42	14
2003	80	50	46
2004	74	46	24
2005	73	36	20
2006	74	37	21
2007	74	34	24
2008	70	35	40
Source: Pew Research Center, December 2008			

For young people, however, the Internet now rivals television as a main source of national and international news. Nearly six-in-ten Americans younger than 30 (59%) say they get most of their national and international news online; an identical percentage cites television. In September 2007, twice as many young people said they relied mostly on television for news than mentioned the Internet (68% vs. 34%).

Main News Source for Young People (% of Respondents Age 18 to 29; Multiple Response OK)				
Main News Source	Aug 2006	Sept 2007	Dec 2008	Change 07-08
Television	62%	68%	59%	-11
Internet	32	34	59	+25
Newspaper	29	23	28	+5
Radio	16	13	18	+5
Magazine	1	-	4	+4
Other	3	5	6	+1
Source: Source: Pew Research Center, December 2008				

According to the Audit Bureau of Circulations for the 6 months ending March 31, 2009, newspapers are losing readers at a still surprising pace. Here are the numbers:

The New York Times -3.5%

The Washington Post -1.6%

USA Today -7.4%

The Chicago Tribune -7.4%

The Los Angeles Times -6.5%

The Boston Globe -13.6%

The New York Daily News -14%

New York Post -20%

The Miami Herald -15.8%

The San Francisco Chronicle -15.7%

The Philadelphia Inquirer -13.7%

The Houston Chronicle -14%

All of the above charts and stats paint a picture that shows a shifting environment for all media customers, vendors and owners.

The people who are spending the money (the ad agencies) also see a clear shift in the growth prospects of where they make their money. As a wise man once told me, it's always important to follow the money.

As we continue to move forward with technology as an ever increasing portion of our lives, the business models that make up this economy will continue to evolve. Will people twitter their way to broadcast all their personal information? Will you pay for news stories digitally? Will people stop buying hard copy books and just get a digital reader? If so, will you pay the same for the book? Will people watch traditional TV or just seek out videos online or get dvd's from netflix or amazon?

Rarely has any prognosticator predicted such wild shifts in the landscape and been proven correct more than 10% of the time.

I will not make predictions either, but I will gladly live and watch and learn.

E-Voter Institute Highlight on Best Web Sites for Political Ads

News-related sites are seen as most effective by consultants for incumbents to reach voters, and sites that attract younger voters are seen as most effective for challengers.

Politically oriented sites, news sites, and search engines are seen as the most effective Internet sources to advertise about incumbent candidates. Sites appealing to young voters, social networking sites, political sites and blogs are believed to be most successful for advertising about challengers.

Best Sites to Promote Incumbent Candidates	
Types of Sites	**Total Consultants**
Political sites	30%
Newspaper sites	24%
Search engines	23%
TV, radio, or cable related sites	22%
Sites that appeal to older voters	21%
Sites that appeal to younger voters	20%
Large portal sites with mass audience	16%
Blogs	16%
Social networking sites	16%
Online video sites	16%
Male oriented sites	14%
Sites based on ethnicity	13%
Female oriented sites	12%
Sites based on religious interests	11%
General interest sites like travel, weather, entertainment, lifestyle	9%

2008 E-Voter Institute Seventh Annual Survey of Political and Advocacy Communications Leaders

Best Sites to Promote Challengers	
Type of Site	**Total Consultants**
Sites that appeal to younger voters	30%
Social networking sites	29%
Political sites	26%
Blogs	26%
Search engines	24%
Online video sites	23%
Newspaper sites	22%
Large portal sites with mass audience	19%
TV, radio, or cable related sites	18%
Female oriented sites	17%
Sites based on ethnicity	16%
Sites that appeal to older voters	15%
Male oriented sites	11%
Sites based on religious interests	11%
General interest sites like travel, weather, entertainment, lifestyle	10%

2008 E-Voter Institute Seventh Annual Survey of Political and Advocacy Communications Leaders

CHAPTER 28

Message Testing in the Age of Rapid Response

Glenn Kessler

The election of 2008 and the preceding campaign season demonstrated how instrumental the Internet can be in mobilizing voters, fundraising for political campaigns, and influencing public opinion. The Internet has become an incredibly powerful and indispensable tool not only for traditional advertisers and marketers, but also for a wide range of interested individuals, groups, and organizations limited only by their own creativity and resourcefulness.

However, despite the evident power of message propagation via the Internet, questions have been raised about political ad-testing:

- In an age where political advertisements can easily be produced and rapidly disseminated on a mass scale by media consultants (due in large part to the advent and subsequent rise of social media), how important is message-testing before the initial release of the advertisement?
- Is campaign money being effectively utilized on

advertisements that resound with voters?

- Are advertisements being effectively tailored and released to their target publics?
- Are traditionally televised political advertisements cost-effective?

Using the MediaCurves.com® advertising testing method and the resulting Political Communications Impact Score (PCIS), a metric score system developed by HCD Research, we can gauge the efficacy of communications such as debates, speeches, and various political advertisements. Consequently, we can see how a particular ad affected specific segments of a sample group.

On August 1, 2008, John McCain released an advertisement entitled "The One," which portrayed Barack Obama's following as little more than celebrity-induced-fanaticism, and questioned his ability to lead. After testing the advertisement, the data shows that the ad not only failed to garner support for John McCain amongst potential swing-voters (i.e. self-reported independents), but may also have strengthened opposition amongst registered Democrats *and* alienated registered Republicans.

Which of the following best describes your overall opinion of John McCain in the 2008 Presidential Election?

Prior to Viewing Ad		After Viewing Ad	
Democrats		Democrats	
Very Favorable	5%	Very Favorable	4%
Mostly Favorable	11%	Mostly Favorable	15%
Mostly Unfavorable	44%	Mostly Unfavorable	29%
Very Unfavorable	41%	Very Unfavorable	53%

Republicans		Republicans	
Very Favorable	34%	Very Favorable	33%
Mostly Favorable	47%	Mostly Favorable	42%
Mostly Unfavorable	14%	Mostly Unfavorable	16%
Very Unfavorable	5%	Very Unfavorable	9%

Independents		Independents	
Very Favorable	8%	Very Favorable	7%
Mostly Favorable	37%	Mostly Favorable	31%
Mostly Unfavorable	26%	Mostly Unfavorable	29%
Very Unfavorable	30%	Very Unfavorable	31%

Amongst Undecided Voters:

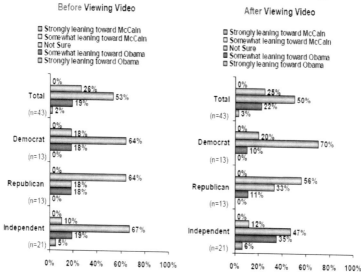

If respondent indicated they are undecided:
"We understand that you are undecided; which of the following best describes your position between voting for John McCain and Barack Obama?"

Percentages may not equal 100 due to rounding

The data indicates that one of the most important groups of voters, the so-called 'undecideds,' responded in an undesirable manner to the McCain campaign ad. Whether the intention of the advertisement was to 'stir up' the Republican base or convert undecided voters, it failed on both accounts. Conversely, McCain's ad "Pump," released July 23, 2008 had more success overall in affecting survey respondents. The data for this study represents a 4% overall preference shift in McCain's favor.

Barack Obama released an advertisement entitled 'New Energy' in the summer of 2008 in response to attack ads launched by the Republican National Committee. The advertisement links McCain to President Bush's energy policies while bolstering Obama's stance as innovative and progressive. After viewing the ad, Obama's favorability amongst all demographics in the sample group increased:

Which of the following best describes your overall opinion of Barack Obama in the 2008 Presidential Election?

Prior to Viewing Ad		After Viewing Ad	
Democrats		**Democrats**	
Very Favorable	50%	Very Favorable	54%
Mostly Favorable	36%	Mostly Favorable	33%
Mostly Unfavorable	10%	Mostly Unfavorable	8%
Very Unfavorable	4%	Very Unfavorable	5%
Republicans		**Republicans**	
Very Favorable	6%	Very Favorable	6%
Mostly Favorable	15%	Mostly Favorable	17%
Mostly Unfavorable	32%	Mostly Unfavorable	32%
Very Unfavorable	48%	Very Unfavorable	46%
Independents		**Independents**	
Very Favorable	12%	Very Favorable	6%
Mostly Favorable	44%	Mostly Favorable	17%
Mostly Unfavorable	25%	Mostly Unfavorable	32%
Very Unfavorable	19%	Very Unfavorable	46%

Conversely, an anti-McCain advertisement was released by Brave New PAC and Democracy for America, implying that John McCain was a poor candidate due to numerous health concerns and a complex medical history. Obama's favorability after viewing the ad, as reported by respondents, was reduced 2% amongst Democrats, 2% amongst Republicans, and 4% amongst Independents. Ironically, McCain's favorability increased 1% overall after viewing the ad.

These particular case studies aptly demonstrate how message testing is an important aspect of an ad's success in effectively persuading a target audience. Conducting comprehensive market research to gauge audience reception and/or interpretation of a particular ad's message may contribute greatly to the successful management of a candidate's image, campaign, and reputation. Moreover, because of the use of Internet panel surveys in market research and message-testing, large studies may be conducted to gauge audience response to an advertisement in a relatively short time-period.

Additionally, obtaining this data prior to the release of an advertisement would allow campaign advisors to make important decisions about the most effective allocation of campaign resources:

- Is the ad, in its current form, worth releasing to a general audience?
- Is it a smart media buy?
- In which markets will the ad be most effective? (i.e. battleground states, a Republican/Democrat saturated region, etc.)

Political ad message testing is a powerful tool in the arsenal of strategies to be utilized by campaign managers and media consultants. It can give a candidate a strategic advantage in close voting battles (such as the recent Al Franken vs. Norm Coleman senate race), help campaigns make more effective and targeted appeals, and act as insurance when second chances to persuade are unavailable.

It would seem that, in future elections, the fast-pace of the modern campaign trail will further contribute to the use of online methodologies. Online surveys will be used to gauge public opinion of media that shape perceptions of a candidate. In a race where few votes decide a victor, the time and expense of a recount and a potential loss may prove to be a powerful incentive to closely and carefully manage a political campaign's communications via the Internet.

Written with support from Mike Logan.

CHAPTER 29

Targeting Diverse Constituents

Karen A.B. Jagoda

The E-Voter Institute 2008 survey asked consultants to indicate the effectiveness of different methods for reaching voters. Standard targeting goals include finding voters by geographic location, gender and ethnicity. What follows are opinions, broken out by party affiliation of the consultants, addressing each of these target audiences.

All Politics is Local

E-Voter Institute 2008 research asked consultants how their strategy differs according to where possible voters live. Looking at voters geographically reveals a different sense of who might be influenced by the Internet with a strong impact seen by consultants in urban areas and almost as much power in suburban areas.

Methods Effective Reaching Urban Voters				
Methods	**Total Consultants**	**Dem**	**Rep**	**Ind**
E-mail	77%	74%	81%	82%
Candidate web site	71%	74%	75%	79%
TV/Cable ads	65%	76%	62%	76%
Events with candidate or surrogate	65%	69%	62%	61%
Social networking sites	64%	65%	65%	66%
Word of mouth	61%	66%	60%	61%
Debates	60%	65%	62%	63%
Blogs and podcasts	59%	60%	60%	63%
Online video	56%	61%	60%	68%
Radio ads	54%	60%	52%	61%
Text messaging	54%	52%	57%	53%
Online ads	53%	56%	54%	50%
Webcasts	53%	54%	52%	61%
Direct mail	51%	58%	49%	55%
Phone	45%	56%	38%	53%
Newspaper ads	40%	45%	35%	47%
Yard signs/outdoor billboards	35%	37%	32%	45%

E-Voter Institute 2008 Seventh Annual Survey of Political and Advocacy Communications Leaders

Methods Effective Reaching Suburban Voters				
Methods	Total Consultants	Dem	Rep	Ind
E-mail	74%	72%	78%	79%
TV/Cable ads	71%	79%	70%	76%
Candidate web site	70%	71%	76%	71%
Events with candidate or surrogate	65%	66%	65%	66%
Radio ads	62%	69%	62%	68%
Direct mail	62%	66%	65%	61%
Word of mouth	60%	63%	63%	66%
Yard signs/outdoor billboards	60%	60%	60%	63%
Debates	58%	61%	60%	61%
Phone	56%	64%	44%	55%
Online ads	52%	54%	49%	42%
Online video	52%	57%	52%	61%
Blogs and podcasts	49%	50%	48%	58%
Social networking sites	49%	53%	40%	50%
Newspaper ads	43%	48%	43%	50%
Webcasts	37%	38%	35%	45%
Text messaging	31%	31%	25%	34%

E-Voter Institute 2008 Seventh Annual Survey of Political and Advocacy Communications Leaders

Methods Effective Reaching Rural Voters				
Methods	Total Consultants	Dem	Rep	Ind
Direct mail	72%	75%	70%	71%
Radio ads	71%	75%	70%	71%
Word of mouth	70%	71%	68%	76%
TV/Cable ads	69%	73%	68%	71%
Phone	62%	67%	57%	66%
Events with candidate or surrogate	57%	59%	57%	63%
Yard signs/outdoor billboards	56%	57%	54%	61%
Debates	56%	60%	57%	50%
E-mail	51%	50%	63%	63%
Newspaper ads	51%	49%	57%	50%
Candidate web site	48%	56%	46%	42%
Online ads	29%	31%	30%	24%
Online video	24%	32%	21%	37%
Blogs and podcasts	19%	21%	16%	21%
Social networking sites	17%	19%	11%	13%
Text messaging	11%	11%	10%	16%
Webcasts	9%	9%	8%	11%

E-Voter Institute 2008 Seventh Annual Survey of Political and Advocacy Communications Leaders

Gender Differences

According to E-Voter Institute 2008 research, consultants indicate that Internet tools affect men and women equally, with some disagreement between those who work with Democratic candidates and those who work with Republican and Independent candidates.

Methods Effective Reaching Men				
Methods	**Total Consultants**	**Dem**	**Rep**	**Ind**
E-mail	67%	65%	76%	74%
Word of mouth	59%	62%	57%	63%
Events with candidate or surrogate	58%	61%	54%	55%
TV/Cable ads	58%	64%	54%	66%
Candidate web site	57%	64%	56%	53%
Direct mail	54%	59%	51%	58%
Radio ads	54%	58%	51%	61%
Debates	53%	57%	49%	42%
Phone	42%	50%	37%	45%
Online video	41%	47%	44%	45%
Newspaper ads	39%	41%	37%	45%
Online ads	38%	43%	43%	34%
Blogs and podcasts	38%	41%	40%	37%
Yard signs/outdoor billboards	38%	42%	33%	50%
Social networking sites	37%	41%	32%	34%
Webcasts	31%	36%	30%	32%
Text messaging	26%	27%	29%	29%

E-Voter Institute 2008 Seventh Annual Survey of Political and Advocacy Communications Leaders

Methods	Total Consultants	Dem	Rep	Ind
E-mail	66%	66%	73%	74%
Word of mouth	65%	68%	67%	66%
Events with candidate or surrogate	62%	65%	59%	55%
TV/Cable ads	59%	65%	60%	68%
Candidate web site	58%	64%	57%	47%
Direct mail	57%	64%	52%	63%
Debates	54%	56%	56%	42%
Social networking sites	51%	53%	49%	45%
Phone	49%	59%	40%	47%
Radio ads	49%	55%	48%	53%
Online ads	38%	44%	40%	34%
Yard signs/outdoor billboards	37%	41%	35%	50%
Online video	37%	46%	37%	39%
Blogs and podcasts	32%	35%	27%	26%
Newspaper ads	31%	36%	30%	42%
Text messaging	30%	31%	30%	34%
Webcasts	27%	27%	25%	24%

E-Voter Institute 2008 Seventh Annual Survey of Political and Advocacy Communications Leaders

Ethnicity

The 2008 E-Voter Institute survey asked political consultants about the best ways to reach blue collar, Hispanic/Latino, and African-American voters. Comparing their answers reveals that the Internet is not seen as a strong tool for reaching any of these groups though candidate web sites and email are seen as important. Do the consultants really understand the online habits of these groups or are they making assumptions?

Methods Effective Reaching Blue Collar Workers				
Methods	Total Consultants	Dem	Rep	Ind
Direct mail	69%	73%	68%	74%
TV/Cable ads	67%	73%	60%	61%
Word of mouth	66%	66%	70%	74%
Radio ads	63%	66%	62%	61%
Phone	62%	65%	54%	66%
Events with candidate or surrogate	57%	59%	56%	53%
Yard signs/outdoor billboards	53%	56%	49%	61%
Debates	39%	41%	38%	32%
Newspaper ads	38%	37%	35%	34%
Candidate web site	38%	45%	33%	47%
E-mail	35%	34%	40%	39%
Online ads	19%	21%	22%	29%
Social networking sites	19%	19%	17%	26%
Online video	18%	20%	22%	29%
Blogs and podcasts	12%	12%	8%	18%
Webcasts	11%	12%	14%	21%
Text messaging	10%	10%	6%	11%

E-Voter Institute 2008 Seventh Annual Survey of Political and Advocacy Communications Leaders

Methods Effective Reaching African-Americans				
Methods	**Total Consultants**	**Dem**	**Rep**	**Ind**
Word of mouth	69%	69%	70%	68%
TV/Cable ads	63%	70%	60%	63%
Radio ads	60%	64%	62%	63%
Events with candidate or surrogate	58%	64%	49%	53%
Direct mail	53%	59%	49%	58%
Phone	51%	59%	40%	50%
Yard signs/outdoor billboards	47%	49%	48%	53%
Candidate web site	43%	51%	41%	58%
E-mail	40%	40%	43%	42%
Debates	35%	42%	29%	29%
Social networking sites	29%	31%	29%	37%
Online video	28%	28%	33%	37%
Online ads	25%	29%	32%	32%
Newspaper ads	23%	24%	21%	16%
Text messaging	20%	22%	17%	26%
Blogs and podcasts	13%	17%	10%	21%
Webcasts	11%	12%	16%	21%

E-Voter Institute 2008 Seventh Annual Survey of Political and Advocacy Communications Leaders

In 2007 and in 2008, E-Voter Institute asked consultants how best to reach Hispanic/Latino voters. Consultants are seeing a growing impact of phone and email, as well as increasing effectiveness of online tools such as the candidate web site and online ads and web video.

Methods Effective Reaching Latinos/Hispanics

Methods	2007 Total Consultants	2008 Total Consultants	Dem	Rep	Ind
Word of mouth	73%	69%	69%	68%	71%
TV/Cable ads	69%	65%	72%	57%	61%
Radio ads	60%	60%	65%	59%	63%
Direct mail	56%	57%	63%	51%	66%
Events with candidate or surrogate	63%	54%	58%	51%	61%
Phone	44%	53%	62%	41%	50%
Yard signs/outdoor billboards	47%	44%	48%	41%	50%
Candidate web site	36%	42%	51%	41%	58%
E-mail	31%	41%	42%	41%	47%
Debates	33%	34%	39%	27%	29%
Newspaper ads	34%	33%	36%	32%	34%
Social networking sites	23%	31%	36%	30%	34%
Online ads	23%	29%	33%	38%	45%
Online video	23%	29%	30%	35%	39%
Text messaging	17%	24%	23%	22%	29%
Blogs and podcasts	14%	17%	20%	13%	24%
Webcasts	13%	12%	13%	17%	29%

E-Voter Institute 2008 Seventh Annual Survey of Political and Advocacy Communications Leaders

PART VI
The Future

CHAPTER 30

Top Ten
Trends

Karen A.B. Jagoda

Future changes in technology will lead to the continuing reordering of how we find out about news, purchase goods and services and interact with friends, professional colleagues, and family. What does this mean for the way citizens prioritize their news-gathering time, how they respond to candidate and advocacy messages, and ultimately vote?

There are many predictions sprinkled throughout this book. This final list is intended to leave you with something more to think about as you consider running for office, managing a campaign, working with an activist group, or consulting to campaigns in 2010 and beyond. You may be studying political science, history, the Internet, or simply interested in national, state, or local campaigns, in which case this list may give you a hint of the broader evolving picture.

Some specifics to keep in mind:

1. Rate of change is accelerating.

We have just started to see the significant changes that the Internet and related technology will bring about in politics, advocacy and government and that change is accelerating. The rate at which new online products and services come onto the market is increasing which requires that candidates, campaign managers and advocates need to learn to adapt faster or risk getting run over.

2. Expectations of voters are increasing.

Changing expectations of voters as consumers of information will drive the way campaigns spend their time and resources and alter the way messages are crafted. Some voters may want short bursts of information in real time, some might prefer the long form of a speech or webcast on demand. Candidates will need to participate in all dimensions with multiple input throughout the day.

3. Megaphones get louder.

Online tools used in national and state-wide races will rapidly migrate down to local races. A critical mass of constituents who are active online will have outsized impact on races and public debate. Expect the accelerated growth of Astro-turf activities in addition to genuine grassroots efforts. The coarsening of the conversation in public meetings and rallies may be fueled by what is seen as acceptable behavior online and voters translating that back to civic discourse in real time real life encounters.

4. Convergence means engagement anywhere and everywhere.

The convergence of phone, computer, and television results in a wider range of devices for reaching voters. This changing media environment will require campaign consultants and managers to consider how messages will play on vastly different screens, in environments with varying light and ambient sound, and varying amounts of time for the voter to listen to or watch a message. The 30-second television ad will soon seem quaint.

5. The King is dead long live the King.

We are already seeing the death and rebirth of traditional ways of running campaigns. Companies will perish, be acquired, form new alliances, or reinvent themselves in the face of changing business demands. The Internet agenda will determine the rest of the media strategy. Those media companies who still treat the Internet as an add-on to their business will be the most vulnerable to the hungry new shops setting up.

6. The Internet becomes a mass medium.

The Internet will increasingly engage all voters. We will see the aging of social nets as more people over 35 leave jobs and seek to maintain relationships. The more a particular social net becomes mass, the more people will look for other online social environments that are cooler and more representative of their own interests. We also need to remember that as more elderly voters die, they are replaced with new voters who are growing up with the web integrated into their entire lives. Expect those on the Internet to get more sophisticated about politics and advocacy as each election cycle passes.

7. The Internet becomes the best way to target.

Campaigns will increasingly be able to target voters online. At the same time, concerns about privacy, behavioral tracking, permission-based communications, and digital profiles will force campaigns to make decisions that maintain the level of trust they have established with voters. Expect competitors to become more sophisticated about targeting each other's base in the search and social network environments.

8. Sources of funding will be hard to track.

Identifying the source of the funds for political and advocacy ads will be an issue as short form ads do not easily lend themselves to such clarifications. Supporters behind Twitter campaigns, search ads and emerging ad forms on social networks will test the rules about disclaimers as the election boards try to define how these ads should be treated. Advocacy groups, lobbyists and non-profit organizations will step up their use of online tools to better cover their tracks.

9. Diversity of elected officials will reflect diversity of citizens.

The faces of elected officials will change. Diversity of candidates including women, minorities, and the disabled will increase and will be supported by web activists. The web is leveling the playing field with new faces able to get recognition using cost-effective online tools to achieve more parity with incumbents. Expect some competitive push-back from those traditional political consultants who don't like the fact that the rules are changing.

10. Metrics will rule the day.

Economic model will be tested and metrics will become more sophisticated. Raising money from big-donors and small will be difficult in the next election cycle or two because of the economy and the choices people need to make about what and who they can support. Return on investment in television, web, direct mail, phone and related advertising venues will be scrutinized. Web standards of tracking will be applied to more traditional methods and campaigns will look beyond just polling and dollars raised to measure success. As a result, the web will see more advertising dollars spent on ad banners, search, streaming audio and video, and email.

How will these changes affect the political campaign process in years to come? Go to our web site: evoterinstitute.com to let us know what you think.

Breinigsville, PA USA
26 October 2009
226484BV00002B/1/P